GROWTH
in the
WILDERNESS

NATALIA HATTON

WESTBOW
PRESS®
A DIVISION OF THOMAS NELSON
& ZONDERVAN

WestBow Press books may be ordered through booksellers or by contacting:

WestBow Press
A Division of Thomas Nelson & Zondervan
1663 Liberty Drive
Bloomington, IN 47403
www.westbowpress.com
1 (866) 928-1240

ISBN: 978-1-5127-2995-5 (sc)
ISBN: 978-1-5127-2996-2 (hc)
ISBN: 978-1-5127-2994-8 (e)

Library of Congress Control Number: 2016901891

Print information available on the last page.

WestBow Press rev. date: 2/15/2016

To all those who are God's precious "work in progress" too

PREFACE

My husband and I walked a hard and long road of infertility, and during that time, I was broken and lost. In 2012 I published *A Mum in Waiting*, which showed a very raw and real account of the eight-year journey to that point. From there a blog was born for the road to follow, and within the words you can see growth taking place. God so lovingly and purposefully picked up the pieces and started mending my entire being.

The words within the pages of this book show the journey walked over the three years of the blog's life. There were more treatments and losses to grapple with. The pain and navigating weren't easy. But all along you can see God's mighty hand at work and the way He transformed as only He can.

At the eleven-year mark on the journey, while our arms remained empty, my heart was far from it. During this juncture, the blog wrapped up as God purposed a new chapter. Not wanting to lose those ups and downs that may encourage and challenge others, I've placed them in this work. You can see the growth God brings, even from what feels like a vast wilderness.

You are about to embark on the blogs that take you on a portion of our infertility journey, my spiritual growth and more. However it would seem unfair to have you on the back foot as most who came to the blog had either read an article that shared some of the first eight years of the journey or had read the book *A Mum in Waiting* so knew the background.

Allow me to take you on a brief synopsis of the first eight years –

- August 2004 we started trying to conceive and have a family.
- 2007 we finally got through the wait list after two years of tests and waiting to see a specialist and found I had endometriosis, resulting in my first surgery to remove it.
- 2009 we went to a natural fertility clinic and tried detoxes, Chinese-herbs, charting, acupuncture and life style changes. This is where we conceived but experienced losses with them not holding.
- 2010 I had my second surgery for endometriosis, we found a fantastic doctor through a private clinic and started Metformin to deal with Poly Cystic Ovarian Syndrome (PCOS). This saw my quality of life altered for the worse during the fifteen months I was on it, seeing us endure great hardship.
- 2011 we paid for a private round of IVF which was a big step for us, sadly both embryo transfers failed. Also a year I was broken, but where I started going to an in depth bible study and God started loving me back to life.
- 2012 we decided to take a break so my body could recover physically and emotionally, which is when God saw me action the first book
- Other key things to note are my childhood of sexual abuse, but a marriage that is solid and God given to help love me back to life and wholeness.

The Big Moment: August 31, 2012

The big moment has arrived to launch *A Mum in Waiting,* and it's with so many mixed emotions that I reach this point.

There is such excitement that all the hard work and sleepless nights are now over with the completion and launch of the book. It's such a huge accomplishment.

I'm hopeful that many will read the book and find something to encourage and help them in whatever they face.

Then, of course, there is the natural side of being scared. I'm putting myself out there like never before, making myself vulnerable with the innermost pain and experiences of such a private journey.

Those Hard Milestones: September 4, 2012

Today I'm turning thirty-three!

Normally, I love birthdays. Brett, my wonderful husband, and I generally go away on some fun getaway. Although I get spoiled when my man gives me awesome presents and we enjoy great food, the best part of all is just time with my favorite person. Family and friends also send their well-wishes and shower me with treats, which are always nice.

This year, as the time approached, I felt dread. I didn't want to celebrate my birthday. I didn't want to acknowledge it was happening—not because I'm one of those people who hates getting older; age in itself isn't the factor. But turning thirty-three felt like I was getting over that hump of having time on my side and getting dangerously close to the big thirty-five, where life starts turning to gloom in the fertility world, as doctors always say age is on your side until thirty-five. Again I'm grateful we started trying when I was twenty-four otherwise it could be an even scarier prospect. This birthday seemed to bring such sadness instead of celebrations, highlighting the fact that my deepest longing is still so far from being a reality.

In my dread, I told Brett I didn't want to go away this year. I told family and friends that I just wanted the day to go by under the radar. I was struggling too much and didn't want to face the birthday. Life felt easier that way.

Then when the day was here, I awoke to amazing presents from my man as well as messages and deliveries flooding in from my family and friends. It seemed they'd forgotten what "under the radar" means, but in a way, I was grateful, because instead of dread, I could turn the birthday around and look at it from a new perspective.

Today the sun is shining with a beautiful rainbow in the sky. I choose to take that as God's personal reminder to me on this day that He has not forgotten His promise to me and that He is my faithful God.

Those special people in my world love me. That fact is a huge blessing and something not to be taken for granted.

Although there is still such an ache of sadness in the pit of my being, this day marks a new year ahead. It is a day full of hope, possibilities, and potential, a blank canvas to start afresh.

So, thirty-three, what do you have for me?

Whirlwind Times: September 20, 2012

When I look back over the last three weeks, I can't believe all that happened, and I can see why it feels like I'm looking at someone else's life instead of my own.

It all started when the proof arrived, and I held it in my hands, exclaiming to Brett over the phone that this experience was surreal. How could this be real? Surely, no ordinary person takes it on herself to write a book—and such a personal one at that.

Before I could reflect too much on that, I was all go with the launch, as the website went live and was available for anyone who desired to read it. There was a big article in the *Herald*, which is New Zealand's national newspaper, and we became inundated with lovely messages from so many people—offers of treatment, words of encouragement, and so much more. If that wasn't big enough, the phone started ringing with other interested media—we are still waiting to see how those requests progresses—and big-time global book distributors contacted us to stock the book. The book was taking off in a way I never expected; I couldn't catch my breath.

We were exhausted from such an intense lead-up to all this and had decided a break away would be a great idea, booking it just before the launch and not realizing how full things ahead would be. Having never been on an island holiday before, we decided now was the time to go and actually relax and unwind. It turns out that even when exhausted, we're not the best at relaxing, so the three days away were certainly all we needed. We packed in some adventures as well, with the awesome tour where you drove a go-kart; we went through jungles, villages, and beaches and saw so much.

My man is the best part of my life, and I loved having such concentrated time with him. My heart swelled with love, pride, and joy as we hung out, and I felt so very blessed with all we shared. There is no better person to share life with.

One night in the stillness at the resort, my mind no longer raced with all the jobs that needed to be done, all the messages I needed to respond to, and whatever else was on my to-do list. I had a moment to catch my breath, and that was when the enormousness of having the book out there hit me. Our very personal journey was now revealed for all to see. It was like my journal, my innermost struggles and thoughts, and my weaknesses and flaws were on display.

The niggles of a rather negative Kindle review started to get the better of me, and I questioned whether that person was right and whether I had messed up in making myself so vulnerable. After all, I don't have the thickest of skin, and words affect me more than some realize. My breathing quickened, and a sense of sheer panic and regret came over me. What had I done? But there was no turning back now. Just at that moment, the stillness and reassurance of God came over me. I could trust Him and would take this journey one step at a time. Joshua 1:9 says, "Have I not commanded you? Be strong and courageous. Do not be terrified, do not be discouraged, for the Lord your God will be with you wherever you go."

I arrived home to my two orders of books and got the blog posting under way. Then I went on to the many e-mails to deal with, and finally, I went on Facebook. Seeing the love and support was amazing. I loved the messages from those who needed a book like this, just as I had. I am so excited about those women who have reached out to catch up. I can't wait to be a listening ear for them and help them as they walk their own journey.

World, this is what I have been created to do. I have a heart for people.

Hope Surges Once Again: September 26, 2012

On the weekend, we had a small dinner party at our place, and anniversaries were discussed. Brett and I would celebrate our tenth wedding anniversary in five months, and we were asked how we would celebrate such a milestone. Again, there was that pang of another milestone looming and not being where we thought we would be in terms of a family. I shared that our backup plan was to celebrate with a holiday, but my absolute hope was that I would be sitting at home, touching a rounded belly, and looking at Brett with absolute delight on my face at having reached our dream of becoming parents, with a wee miracle growing inside. When asked what the steps toward that event happening were, I said I would be discussing a third surgery, since my endometriosis was out of control again. Then I was starting Vitamenz and looking at our next round of in vitro fertilization (IVF) once the Vitamenz had worked its magic. It would be a tight timeline, but anything was possible, and with God on our side, I was full of hope.

Yesterday I dropped in to the private fertility clinic to see Neil, our amazing fertility specialist, and the nurses to have a catch-up and hand over the book in person. In passing I mentioned the need to make an appointment to discuss another surgery, as the pain was out of control again. It simply couldn't wait for our "year of fun" to be over and needed to be addressed. Neil knew I hadn't wanted another surgery; with my last one, I'd wanted us to have our much-wanted miracle before another surgery was even contemplated. I had wanted my next surgery to be a full hysterectomy, but alas, things don't always go according to plan. An appointment was made, and a new discovery of injections rather than surgery was mentioned.

I am so full of hope as we await the appointment and see where to go from here. Please, God, may this be our turning point. May we celebrate our tenth wedding anniversary with a double miracle on board and close this chapter of our lives once and for all.

Those Little Boosts: October 2, 2012

I felt a bit flat this morning after someone said some discouraging words to me and once again thought we were at a crossroads I would rather do without. I was over walking this journey and just wanted off this enforced roller coaster ride. Thankfully it was the same day my amazing friend and I had planned to have a girls' morning, as it was just the boost I needed.

Off I went to Nat's, and from there we headed to Newmarket. With her second on the way, we discussed extras for the pram so her toddler could ride along with the newborn. I suggested that we check out the store on Manukau Road, one I had always admired and longed to go into when our turn came. I had wandered into baby stores in the malls by myself, but this was a specialist store that required one to park and intentionally go in. I'd always felt like a fraud if I did that, so I had eagerly awaited my moment, not realizing it would come sooner than expected. Well, it was a glimpse at least.

Nat was busy with the shop assistant, trying out various contraptions for the buggy and discussing all the ins and outs of it. This was my moment to quietly wander around the store. My eyes caught all the sweet little all-in-ones and spotted the amazing buggies, the soft toys, and all the special things scattered about this beautiful store. I felt my heart boost as I thought of the excitement I would have when that day came for us to come in here and buy up all the baby gear. I could feel my eyes well up with happy tears and was overcome with emotion.

Getting out my phone, I texted Brett, "I finally got to go in Global Baby cos I'm with Nat. Love the store! So excited I want to cry. Can't wait, my babe!" My hope, faith, and expectation once again surged. The doubts, frustrations, and emotions I'd felt because of others' words and the crossroads we faced were once again pushed to the side.

I don't know what keeps the rest of you going in this journey or what those little boosts are for you, but I for one am so glad this is what my day held, as I really needed it.

Life Keeps Getting Better: October 11, 2012

On Saturday night we were blessed with an amazing fine-dining degustation dinner, which Vitamenz put on in our home. We not only spent the night with some of our most favorite people in the world but also got to meet some absolute legends in Aaron and Kirsty.

The following day we enjoyed some Mexican and a yarn with Aaron and his wife, Jacinta. Speaking with people who had walked the journey and really understood it was amazing. I felt like we had known them for years, with the ease of it all.

During that dinner Jacinta mentioned phoning the coordinator for publicly funded IVF, as it seemed crazy that we still hadn't heard a thing on when our publicly funded cycle of IVF would be. Nineteen months had passed without a word, and we had heard of others being contacted after just a few months. I had already decided to seek the coordinator, but given the lumps in my left breast and the impending mammogram, I was waiting till I knew we didn't have a battle of another kind on our hands.

On Monday morning my mammogram gave me the all clear on not following in the family history footsteps; rather, the breast was riddled with cysts, which wasn't a concern. They were just painful. Right. That meant I could phone the lovely nurse at the private fertility clinic and see what I was supposed to do. She gave me the ladies' details, and it turned out she was absolutely lovely and on the ball; that was just what I needed.

I seemingly slipped through the cracks, but she hopes to get us into November orientation for a February cycle of IVF. It's just a matter of doing paper work and trying to do the best they can. With them on the case, helping, I have no doubt it will all work out, and I feel a real peace about it.

I am in awe of how God works, of how His timing and ways are perfect. Let me share the points that bring me to this realization:

- If we hadn't slipped through the cracks and been called up for public IVF, with the devastation of losing Steve, a friends husband, to cancer and going through our own year of unthinkable hardships, I'm not sure I could have faced public IVF and not be under Neil's care at the start of this year.
- The book that has helped others and brought amazing people across our path wouldn't have come into being, as my focus would have been elsewhere.
- After my mammogram on Monday, with a male doctor coming in to do the ultrasound, I was proud of myself for not going into panic mode (a history of sexual abuse can cause you to panic when in a dark room alone with a stranger for medical procedures and body parts are exposed). That experience showed me how far I've grown and how much more of my past I've dealt with. That experience gives me such confidence in going into publicly funded IVF and not needing to fear that side of things.

- The crossroads we now face has been taken out of our hands, and we can simply walk forward in this direction with complete peace of mind and be able to do *all* of it.
- Best of all, this process has enabled Brett and me to get some fun and "us" time back in our lives; it has allowed us to heal and be prepared for another intense time.

In the big and small, God is always in control and working for our best, even when we can't see His hand. Today I have such a sense of joy, as I can see Him working, even when others would look at the same picture and see something negative.

Life sure is good, and with every week, it's just getting better and better. I'm one truly blessed and happy girl.

A Brand-New Chapter: October 19, 2012

We had our appointment with our legendary specialist, Neil, yesterday evening. A brand-new chapter in this journey has begun, and I am hopeful and full of anticipation. Once again I can see God's hand in all the comings and goings, and I feel so very blessed by all He is doing.

I had so wanted my second surgery to be my final one before my miracle babies and then follow it with a hysterectomy to be done with the pain and debilitation endometriosis brings to my life on a regular basis. As the months went by this year, it was very apparent that the endometriosis was getting out of control once again, with a third surgery looking inevitable. I'm grateful for great specialists on the ball with new discoveries and possibilities.

Neil informed us that one way to go would indeed be surgery, but as it would be my third, surgeries become less effective and aren't a long-term solution. He discussed having three months of Zoladex injections; a doctor administers these every twenty-eight days, and they basically suppress the effects of endometriosis, as I would be put in early menopause. Studies have also shown that it is a positive lead in to IVF with greater success rates, although the studies are all very new, and there are varying opinions on it all. He went over the pros and cons of the options very thoroughly, including caring in his delivery of it all, and left the decision in our court.

We looked at each other, discussed the matter, and decided "Let's give it a crack." There is always the option of coming off the injections if the side effects prove to be greater than they should be. Clearly my response to Metformin, the drug to help with PCOS, is an indicator that I don't fit in the boxes all too well. But how could my situation really be worse than it was last year, and with the chance of greater success with IVF, the injections seem well worth it. You can always laugh at my getting to experience the hot flashes and menopausal stage of life before all my friends, who are one up on me with their experiences with motherhood. This is my chance to lead the way in one area, at least.

The paper work is also sorted for me to start publicly funded IVF, and it seems that with my points (for public IVF you're eligible based on a point system; for example how long you've been trying, reasons for complications etc), we would be eligible for not one but *three* chances, so that news can mean only good things. We are set to have December orientation with a March cycle. Neil is sending the people in charge of public IVF a letter, listing all my history, which could feel like an undefeatable mountain of opposition. With God on my side, I feel like anything is possible and am looking forward with anticipation and expectation, if I dare to be so bold. It's also nice to know Neil's letter will open the door to an understanding of my history and potentially means we will have the great care we have grown so accustomed to.

I have to admit that it feels a wee daunting to be leaving the care of such an amazing specialist and to venture into an unknown field. However, I'm grateful that we will still be with our trusty team (Neil and the private fertility clinic nurses) when it comes to taking injections, dealing with my endometriosis, and facing my upcoming hysterectomy after having my miracles and possibly taking more fertility care, should the three rounds not suffice. I said to Brett that

I feel like I'd want to make appointments during our publicly funded treatment just to see how they are going and to update them on our journey, as they have been such an integral part. However, our pockets will be grateful to have a breather after eight years of paying for private care, and that's the only reason why I'm even venturing out of my nest, so to speak.

We haven't always had the best of luck with the public field, and I can't say I'm not nervous about what lies ahead. But I choose to hold onto what's positive and think of how far we've come and how better prepared we will be should we meet some bumps in the road. It helps that I've heard of some great experiences with the door we are about to venture into, so here's hoping that our experience is good too and that God will once again blow me away with what is in store.

My wonderful mother-in-law, Gail, was just on a trip and brought us back a wee gift of hope. She said to pop it away in our cupboard for our miracle, but we have instead left it out by my bedside. Each day we will be able to look at it and know it signifies a new chapter, one full of new beginnings, brighter hope, greater strength, and many expectations for our bundle of joy.

So here we go, about to embark on the next chapter and praying that 2013 will be our year for a miracle and hopefully a double portion at that. I look forward to having you along for the ride.

A Beaming Self: October 31, 2012

Although this week has been very hectic, with all the hats I wear, it has been wonderful. I caught up with some very amazing friends I don't often see. It was so encouraging to hear that I seemed like my old self. They could see how happy, content, hopeful, and healthy I was after seeing me so different on other occasions. Their words made me realize how far I've come. I'm no longer broken from that most awful year, but rather I'm healed and in a much better way than before. As I told one of them, I feel like I've shut a very heavy and massive door on that chapter and am so excited about venturing into this next one.

Then, to truly top off my day, a lady from the public fertility clinic phoned to check on whether we still required IVF and then booked us for our orientation day. We will not only go through the motions of what doing IVF publicly means on December 4 but also find out when our IVF cycle starts. As I will be on Zoladex, I won't have a "day one," so there will be no wondering when it will be, just a date picked and going straight into it.

I haven't been able to stop beaming all afternoon. I am so full of hope and feel like I'm in the best space I could possibly be in after all we've been through. Taking this year out to process and heal, a year to have fun and do new thing's, was exactly what was needed. Watch this space, people. There is greatness ahead for the Hatton's, whatever that may look like. I am once again ready.

Music That Stirs You: November 6, 2012

This is our year of fun. When we saw Ben Harper was coming to New Zealand, we knew going to his concert had to be part of that year of fun. When Brett and I were in our "just friends" stage all those years ago in our teens, we listened to Ben Harper and Jamiroquai as we drove around in his car. The music is an integral part of many memories and firsts. Last night Brett and I went to the Ben Harper concert in Auckland City. We made a night of it with some great Mexican food too.

As we sat in the ASB Theatre, waiting for the seats to fill and for Ben to come on stage, the excitement swelled. I couldn't wait to hear him live, to see whether he was as good as I expected and what his on-stage presence was like. He didn't disappoint, nor did the music. He is so talented, and his lyrics have a way of evoking memories and stirring emotions.

When "Diamonds on the Inside" started, I had flashbacks to so many memories of us over the years. I looked at my babe and smiled, as I felt so blessed to have grown up with this man. We were just teens, and now look what paths we have walked and the lives we have led. I felt my heart fill with love and pride for the amazing man beside me. How truly blessed I am.

Over the course of the evening, there were many lyrics that evoked emotion. Allowing me to reflect on the grace of God, how life is a mixture of good and bad, which molds us, and how friendships can come to an end. I love how music has the power to evoke memories, to stir emotion, and even to change lives. So many things in our lives can impact us if we let them.

Thanksgiving Day: November 22, 2012

Thursday is the celebration of Thanksgiving Day in America and now in many other places around the world. I remember my first experience of Thanksgiving as a young child in Indonesia. There were many American families, so we had the pleasure of being immersed in all things American: the Fourth of July, Thanksgiving, Christmas at its best, and so much more. The Snell's, who were like our second family as we grew up in Indonesia, were amazing at putting on a celebration and welcoming all. The house was covered in decorations. There was sawdust on the floor, and they were dressed up as pilgrims and Indians, with tables covered in food that was so foreign to me. I was introduced to pumpkin pie, among many other treats. The kids ran in and out of the room, played games, and just had the best time. As the evening grew to a close, we were all called into the main area, and that was when I found out about the meaning behind the fun. They shared the history and said what they were thankful for.

Today I am no longer that little girl with the decorations, food, and Americans I love around me, but I can reflect on the meaning of the day and be thankful for the many blessings in my life.

From the greatest …

- The most amazing husband, who is the best part of my world. He is the love of my life, my best friend, and my absolute favorite person to spend time or life with.
- Our friends and family, who bless us in so many ways just by being them. They also allow us to be part of their world, and in turn they are part of ours.
- Being able to have a real relationship with my God, who is faithful, gracious, and constant. I have also benefited from a church and Bible study, and I have grown into a better person.
- Living in a country that has such beautiful surroundings offers many great experiences and benefits, including a sense of safety. Many places don't offer a society where there are so many great people.
- Having the opportunity of new hope as we approach this next round of treatment and IVF. With something different added to the mix, we are given a greater sense of expectation for our miracle.

To the least …

- My love of food is back, as I once again have the health, energy, and enjoyment for cooking and creating in the kitchen.
- Color brightens my world and brings a smile—from the glistening nails to the fun with MAC or even to the fresh items in my wardrobe.
- In a matter of days, I can set up my Christmas decorations and once again get into the joy of the season, because of being in a much better place than the previous two years.
- Crinkles around my eyes. For many years I admired the beautiful lines around the eyes of others, which to me signified a life lived to its fullest, and at last I have some of my own.
- The fact that summer is coming. That means there is so much fun to be had—water, sand, barbecues, camping, music, friends, and so much more.

I'm one very blessed girl with such a full and happy life. I'm thankful for all my world holds, and I'm excited for the hope of it becoming even greater as we broach 2013.

At a Crossroads: December 4, 2012

Today was orientation for public IVF. I sit here, still processing the morning, unsure how I feel other than deflated. I went into today not expecting the same experience we had under Neil and the private fertility clinic, but we did expect to meet many lovely people and to come away full of anticipation and strengthened hope, with a clear way forward and everything laid out.

We did meet another great team of people, but I haven't come away full of anticipation or a clear way forward. I had thought we would come away with concrete dates on when I would start Zoladex injections and how those would translate to a start date for March IVF. It seems that my expectations and what went down didn't line up.

I'm not sure when I will start Zoladex and for a moment was told that the plan had been changed, but we discussed it back into being. I'm not sure when IVF will start in March, what dose I will be on, or what protocol we will do. I'm left with more questions than answers, and I'm not so great in that situation. I like plans being clear-cut.

There is also the niggling question inside me of how public or private to be with this round of IVF. Clearly I have written a book that lays bare our eight-year journey to date. I even gave the clinic a book to use as a resource on arrival. As we had stints in the waiting area between the various meetings with the doctor, counselor, nurses, and embryologist, I began to feel vulnerable and exposed because of the book's existence. I wondered how it would impact this next chapter we are embarking on. Then we had a moment in the waiting room as a couple whispered about who we were, the *Herald* article, and the book—which just added to my uncertainties and vulnerability as to what to do about this blog.

I'm at a crossroads, as I'm not sure what lies ahead for our IVF cycle, and I'm also unsure of how much to share as we walk the journey.

In the Unknown: January 17, 2013

I'm currently in the middle of my treatment of Zoladex injections as we prepare for our next round of IVF but this time in the public sector, so we will be going to the public hospital instead of the private clinic and not have one set team caring for us but rather whoever is on at the time of procedures and appointments. This certainly is a roller coaster ride, as on the whole I'm so confident and excited, but there are those moments when the unknown of it all feels daunting.

During the Christmas holidays, Brett and I camped up north, and it was absolute bliss. I loved spending time with my wonderful babe, enjoyed exploring the beauty of New Zealand's nature and finally having a holiday, which wasn't so dominated by illness or recovery from this journey. One morning as I lay awake to the sound of birds chirping, stillness in the campground, and water lapping just beyond, my mind turned to our impending IVF cycle. I had been so expectant, so certain that March would be our month, and at long last we could leave this chapter behind. In that quietness it dawned on me that there was actually a significant possibility of this not going according to plan, as if the past eight and a half years hadn't been proof enough of that.

The heavy question lingered—what would I do if this wasn't our time? In the stillness God gently reminded me that none of the situation was on me; it was all on Him, so I should be still and know that He is God. If indeed His timing was yet again not mine, then He would be the one to pick me up, to give me the peace and strength needed to walk forward in hope yet again. I didn't need to find these resources within; I simply needed to look to Him, and He would give me all I needed in that moment.

Now that time has passed and we are fast approaching the start of IVF, I can't help but have those waves of uncertainty, that longing for assurance that this will be it. Instead I try to think back on that gentle reminder from God and rest in that.

Vows: January 28, 2013

"I, Natalia, take you Brett to be my lawfully wedded husband to have and to hold from this day forth. For better or worse, for richer or poorer, in sickness and in health, to love and to cherish until death parts us." —Saturday, February 1, 2003

The day I got married, I was so in love and meant those words with all my heart. But I was young and naïve and couldn't possibly have fathomed what it meant to live them out. Now, as our tenth wedding anniversary is a matter of days away, our vows hold so much more meaning, and my love for my husband is so much deeper and stronger.

On my wedding day, I woke with such excitement, as I was getting ready. I felt so beautiful as I had one last look in the mirror, truly feeling like a princess in a fairy tale. I was getting married to the love of my life, my best friend. It seemed like the beginning of our "happily ever after."

When life doesn't turn out the way you expected or hoped for and when those hardships stretch beyond what you could ever imagine, that is when you truly see those vows in action. In those moments you see what true love is—a husband tirelessly caring for you, going to countless fertility appointments, sleeping in hospitals just to be by your side, fetching ice, rubbing your back, heating heat packs, cooking meals, learning how to inject IVF drugs, holding your hand with each new hurdle, and being a pillar of strength and comfort on those hardest days. Those are the moments when you realize how immensely blessed you are, and you know that no matter what lies ahead, those vows will never just be words. They will hold such weight and give such certainty as you choose to live them out each and every day.

There have been ups and downs with every aspect of life in our ten years of being Mr. and Mrs. Hatton. The constant has been our love for each other and our walking beside one another through it all. As I reflect on the past ten years, the significance of our vows, what my wonderful babe and I share, and all that lies ahead, I'm the happiest and most blessed girl alive. I love being Mrs. Hatton and can't wait to celebrate my tenth wedding anniversary with my man.

When You Look Back: February 12, 2013

On the whole, most people want to look forward, to leave behind the hard moments in their lives. But sometimes when you look back, you see things in a new perspective. That is what happened to me this week as I was thinking about what was ahead of us. I found myself sitting at my desk with my journal in front of me to make a new entry, as I had just had a very encouraging devotional reading I wanted to note down. I felt very weary from my lack of sleep with the side effects and didn't really feel like rushing up from my comfy spot, so I decided to flick back over my journal.

It started with Wednesday, May 23, 2012:

> My old journal finished some time ago, but I didn't want a new one. I just wanted a baby and to have no need for one. This year has been huge in so many ways, from dealing with emotions and hardships to friendships, and even to my grounding in God being rocky.
>
> Through the in-depth Bible study, sermons, devotionals, and people saying things, God has been pulling away the rubble of my broken self and tending to it all.
>
> I can't believe it, but yesterday I finished *A Mum in Waiting* to its final draft. Now Brett, Hannah (a friend and prayer partner), Nat (a friend), and Ben (a friend of a friend who is walking such a road with his wife) are reading it to give me honest feedback. From there it will either be a time-consuming way for me to outlet it all, or we can find a publisher and see if it is publishable and sell it.

I can't wait to see what God does from here, in all aspects to be honest. I finally feel like I can breathe and not feel like such a mess. I can have my deep sense of peace back and start healing and truly move forward, whatever that is and however it looks. Yikes!

I skipped a few entries to Tuesday, June 12, 2012:

Catherine shared T. D. Jakes's speaking on Facebook. Wow! What a timely thing to hear. Here are some notes I jotted down while listening:

— It's not the destination or promise as much as it's about what you learn on the way.
— When you get there, you will talk about the things you learned along the way, what God has done, and how He carried you through the desert place.
— All things work together for *His* good!
— In the desert place, yet will I trust Him!
— Many preachers talk about prosperity, and people think if they trust God and walk with Him, life will be easy and perfect. But you can be in Him, doing His will, and be in hardship. Don't doubt and despair.
— God teaches patience in the hardships. He hasn't forgotten you. He will keep that promise. He hears your cry, but He wants you to stop being hysterical, to be still and know He is God. When that happens, He responds, and your miracle is near.
— He doesn't need you to have it all together. He uses what's broken. In fact, the broken are those whom He brings to impact those who are also broken in the desert and don't have it all together. If you think *you* can be in ministry, then that is when your pride gets in the way, when you are judgmental and do damage. But when you don't think you can is when He uses you and does the work through you to reach others.

— When you look in the rearview mirror you see the grass in the desert, the ways God carried you, how He pulled you through and you avoided what could have been. The small things are just as significant as the destination. Thank Him for the doors that opened and closed. Thank Him for those who stuck by you and the ones who left you. Thank Him for where you are in life and for the miracles that happened along the way.

I now have a greater understanding of Isaiah 48:10 and Psalm 23: how God can turn something from ashes to beauty, how He can shape and use you through the hardships, how He can carry and refine you in those dark days, how He can provide joy and peace in all seasons, and most of all, how He is always present. How about you? If you looked back, would you see your own life through new eyes? Sometimes when we look back, we remember the shelters in the desert or the sweet, significant, life-altering moments that could be achieved only in the storm, those that prepare us for the mountaintops ahead.

When Dreams Mingle with Reality: February 23, 2013

We are fast approaching March, and as we get closer, people are excited for us. I have to admit that until recently, the dominating emotion for me has also been great excitement, anticipation, and hope. I have mainly focused on the longed-for end result and not thought of the actual process and all that entails.

There is that dream of having the life-changing news that we are indeed pregnant with a keeper and having that longing to have a growing belly and to feel our precious miracles wriggle about, that ache for our babies to melt away as we experience the first moment of being parents. Those are all the moments you daydream about and long for as you face another round of treatment. You find yourself daydreaming once again about how you will share the news and what the nursery will look like. You spend hours praying for the children who will be.

Then the day comes when the reality of what you are about to go through hits you like a pile of bricks. You are overwhelmed with so many mixed emotions. The memories of the last round come flooding back as you think about how tender your stomach was, how much you hated those last days of injections, how intrusive the scans and procedures were, and the yoyo emotions you endured with each step. Then you can't help but wonder whether you will once again be devastated and have to pick yourself up or whether this really could be the time when your dreams become reality and this unthinkable journey will be over.

Only my wonderful husband sees what doing IVF really entails and all that is endured. Others see the glossy version of it, where action is happening, and there is once again hope.

I'm grateful that God will once again sustain me, provide me with the strength and hope needed, and pave the way. I'm thankful for a husband who is truly in the thick of it with me; and this is *our* journey, not mine alone. I appreciate those close family and friends who will once again be our champions and walk this chapter with us. But I can't help but feel tender, raw, scared, and self-protective as we are once again about to go through something huge.

The Next Chapter Begins: March 8, 2013

Over the past eight and a half years, this journey has taken us through many highs and lows, with plenty of unexpected twists and turns. Today marks the beginning of new hope in action as we will be collecting the drugs to start what we hope is our final round of IVF.

As you saw from previous posts—"At a Crossroads" and "When Dreams Mingle with Reality"—I was unsure whether to share when our next round started because I was feeling very raw, scared, and protective. If I'm honest, I felt I had laid myself bare enough with the book and was feeling reserved about sharing this next portion.

I've had very little sleep while I've been on Zoladex, with many nights providing under two hours of sleep. In February I hit a wall of exhaustion, which led to the hard point of emotions getting too much for me. Thankfully in the past weeks, God has been encouraging me through the in-depth Bible study, devotionals, and the prayers of my champions. I have seen a real turning point, and once again I'm renewed in my hope, excitement, and anticipation.

Ordinarily with something big like a new round of IVF starting, I would feel the need to gain some control and turn to spring cleaning and exercise. God has clearly been doing some big work in me because I've sold the home exercise machine and haven't done anything beyond my usual housework for the week. There is such a deep sense of peace and a real reliance on Him as we take the step into this next chapter, and even though I don't know what lies ahead, that is finally okay.

So here we go, people. Ready to come along for the ride?

The Resounding Hope: March 11, 2013

There seems to be the continuous reminder of hope with this round of IVF.

The other day I flipped the page over to start that day's devotional, and what do you know but the title was "Abounding in Hope." I read the verse "May the God of hope fill you with all joy and peace in believing, so that by the power of the Holy Spirit you may abound in hope" (Romans 15:13). It goes on to say that as we look around this world, there is a sense of hopelessness; we cannot live without hope, and it comes from God alone. The devotional finished off with this paragraph: "But hope isn't just a future thing. It's a now thing. Hope enables us to live an abundant, joy-filled life in the great right now. We may not see circumstances as hopeful, but because we are connected to the God of the universe, we can ensure them with a paradoxical joy."[1]

A day later I decide to do a blog, wanting to find an image of hope to put in the photo board I was creating. I saw a stone with the word *hope* on it. The words my dear friend Hannah spoke from our last cycle of IVF come flooding back, and I can't help but think how fitting it is that I have found a stone with the word *hope* to mark this cycle.

Then we went to have dinner with our dear friends Nat and Kyle before we started the injections and were given a gift to mark this moment and their support. As I unwrapped it, I saw an angel of hope, and my eyes filled with tears of joy. I'm so thankful that God reminds us of His care each step of the way, and I'm grateful for the people He has put in our path for such a time as this.

There is a ringing in my ears, and that is for hope. There is a constant reminder that God has us in this, and with each step, we have every reason to be thankful and confident.

Are you in need of hope with something you are facing in life? I have every reason to believe that sense of hope can be yours today too.

IVF Brings Out the Giggles: March 14, 2013

To start with, I'll take you back to when I was eight so you get a glimpse into what has formed me or how I'm wired, for better and worse. We were back in Matamata, a small town in New Zealand that is now well known because of a movie, on a visit and had to go to the doctors for blood tests. It was the first blood test I can remember. As a young family having lived in Papua New Guinea and Indonesia, we had already had many injections. I had been very brave with all of those, as I wanted the reward of the doll, ice cream, and whatever else we had been bribed with. But on this particular day, things were a little different. The nurse suggested that my sister go first, as she was older and could show me how the blood test was done. This was a big mistake.

I watched my sister scream bloody murder and cry her eyes out. I decided that the blood test must hurt so bad and wasn't having it. In her defense, the nurse had our dad go first, and we saw the blood coming out into a tube, a sight that isn't ideal for little girls. Anyway, I told my dad I was going to wait outside. He was fine with that, and I slipped out. I didn't plan to wait, though; I dashed out the door and ran all the way to the house where we were staying. I arrived out of breath and my mum asked me where the others were. I told her they were still there and hid under the bed. I don't know why I thought this would stop me from being found and taken back, because before long, my dad arrived, found me, and drove me right back. The nurse bribed me with a treat, which works wonders every time with me, and I sat up on the bed. I looked away at the jar of treats, wondering how many I would be given if I was really brave. I felt a prick and asked when the test was going to be done, as I expected some kind of torture and was thankful to be told it was already over.

Despite the test being easy, I think that moment had given me a fear of needles, and so from then on, I would get really nervous and work myself up, only to find again that the test was no big deal. If you think about how much I hated needles before this eight-and-a-half-year journey, I have to say I am pretty proud of myself for the way I have gotten so good with blood tests, injections, and all the procedures. However, when a professional isn't doing it, it's a whole other ball game again.

This time around there isn't the easy pen for me to do the first lot of injections myself; rather, there's a vile to put a syringe into and draw back on. Then one can put a longer needle into me. When we had our clinic visit and saw this, I told Brett the task was all on him this time, as there was no way I was doing that to myself.

I've had many people ask me how these injections are going this time around, as they've read the book and seen the comical side of IVF. Page 129 in *A Mum in Waiting* says, "On one of the nights I really didn't want the injection and have to admit I ran around the island bench telling Brett, no. I was tired and just didn't feel like the irritation afterward and the pain of it. Rather silly I admit, but thankfully, it made him even quicker. He became a pro and it didn't even hurt after that so there was no need to run around the bench again."

So to answer the question for you curious people, there has been no running around the bench to date. But I guess you should know that I've decided to lie down on the couch to be injected so I can't back away. The first night, I admit, I was nervous and said that I didn't want to have the injection anymore. I kept pulling clothing down to cover my stomach and saying, "No" for a good minute. Brett did an amazing job, given I was nervously giggling, which meant my stomach was moving around. Now that I've managed to stop giggling for the last two nights, he is doing an even better job. The injection is over quickly, and we have the routine down pat.

The other topic I've been asked about is side effects, so let me update you on that too. There are no side effects to date, and I often forget we are even doing IVF till my alarm sounds for the evening injection. We are not into the rhythm of blood tests, phone calls from the clinic, or scans just yet. I still, however, have my Zoladex side effects of hot flashes and insomnia, but I'm hoping those will soon pass.

The Joys of Menopause: March 19, 2013

Over our eight-and-a-half-year journey, I have had many mothers share their words of wisdom with the all-too-often-used phrase "Just wait till you are a mum, and you will get what we mean."

When I've been in the part of the journey I've struggled with, those words have grated on me sometimes. It's not from a lack of trying or choice that I find myself wishing to experience motherhood, which they make seem like an exclusive club.

Well, it's now my moment to share some words of wisdom with you and be able to say, "Just wait till you are older and go through menopause, and then you will get what I mean."

This journey must have its bright points, and I choose to make experiencing menopause as one of those by seeing the humor in it. Now that my treatment of Zoladex has passed and my body no longer seems to be in its three-month experience of menopause, I would like to share some moments with you.

In the appointment with Neil, our specialist, we discussed the new treatment option, with all its pros and cons. He rattled off some possible side effects with Zoladex—hot flashes, sweating, headaches, dizziness, mood changes, sleep problems (insomnia), acne, and itching, among other things.

Neil said that to know it was working, some side effects would be good, so as I left the appointment, I told God I would like to have hot flashes and headaches. After all, with endometriosis I tend to be on the cold side, so I figured I would end up being like others if I was to warm up a bit. Then, due to years of headaches prior to my first surgery, I knew I could handle those—no worries.

Days after the first deposit of Zoladex sat under my skin, ready to disburse over the twenty-eight-day course, the side effects started to kick in. Sure enough, God graciously heard my prayers, and I had the two side effects I had requested and nothing more or less. How silly I was to think that hot flashes would be no big deal and would balance out my body temperature.

With a hot flash, you are overwhelmed with a heat that makes you think your body will self-combust. Your face fills with an intense heat that is like no other, and there doesn't seem to be much you can do about it. It hits you in waves, and for me they were all too regular.

I quickly had to go out and purchase dresses, as my normal wardrobe simply wouldn't suffice. I ate a lot of ice cubes, placed many cold facecloths all over my body, opened all the windows and doors, and had the fan constantly going. I suddenly loved being in the car with the air conditioning blasting and was that crazy person out in public trying to cool down and get airflow. I often forgot what normal people felt and heard people comment about being freezing, thinking they were in Antarctica or something when around me.

The headaches were constant but very manageable. There were a few moments over the three months when my headaches resulted in dizzy spells and nausea, but they weren't too significant to be bothersome. I just had to take it easy during those moments. My hot flashes meant that I got very little sleep, and at times I had heat rashes. But they were all related to the two side effects I had requested.

During the first half of the treatments, I was awake at all hours because of my overheating. I would lie there in the dark and stillness of the night, feeling bad for being up and down, cooling my facecloths, getting ice, and crunching away. I was so thankful that Brett was such a deep sleeper. I spent many hours looking at my phone, as I got so very bored.

During the first week. I remember waking in the middle of the night with my first hot flash. I had the biggest grin on my face and thought better of it, but I really wanted to wake Brett to share my exciting news—the treatment was working, as there were side effects. For many weeks I lay there with a big smile on my face, full of hope because the therapy was doing it's job. I guess it's all about perspective. However, as the weeks became months and an overwhelming sense of exhaustion kicked in, there weren't big smiles; rather there was frustration and a longing for it all to be over.

I began missing my duvet, my normal wardrobe, and my ability to function with good sleep; and I longed for the time to be up. I ended up getting excited about having a good stint of sleep and wanted to wake Brett with that news but always thought better of it. Who would ever think you would rejoice over two hours of sleep? I also found that my auntie was right; I ended up getting dry skin and needed to apply extra moisturizer and get treatments for my hair. It was like the heat dried everything out.

So here are some words of wisdom for when you hit menopause:

- Purchase many cool dresses.
- Eat lots of ice and drink lots of cold water.
- Have cold flannels, fans, and air conditioning on hand.

- Your neck is the most effective place for the facecloth at night.
- Get moisturizes that are rich in vitamins.
- Have cold showers just before leaving the house.
- Get a pedicure that is cooling for the feet as a treat.
- Have something in your bag to fan yourself with in public when the heat hits.

I can't say I know the aggravation of proper menopause, which stretches on for many months and even years. Nor have I had the many other side effects that can come, such as mood swings, but others may be able to fill you in on those factors; and when you're not hoping for a miracle, you are permitted to try all the remedies out there to make it easier.

IVF Is Well Under Way: March 21, 2013

I can't believe it, but somehow today is day twelve of doing injections for IVF. The experience started a little bumpy, with my wanting to retreat from the needle when the clock hit seven each evening. But in all honesty, the process has been smooth sailing, with Brett doing an amazing job with injections, me gritting my teeth to bear it, and only one night when the needle must have hit a nerve. There were tears and a lot of pain. Even introducing the second injection five nights back was no big deal.

One evening we were in the car, heading out, and the alarm sounded for injection time. We laughed at the fact that Brett had thought we didn't need an alarm when I first set it up. After all, how on earth could we forget such a thing, especially with my attention to detail and planning? But forget we did.

It wasn't because we weren't so grateful for being able to do treatment once again, hopeful for the end result in this with all we have. Simply the fact is, this time around is so very different. We don't have that all-consuming desperation, striving, over-thinking, hounding God with questions, bargaining, and pleading.

The deep-seated peace is an absolute reflection of how far God has brought us and of the work He has done in me through our trials and tribulations. There is no other explanation. The reality of going public and not having our trusty specialist should have had me in an absolute state of needing to control things and being consumed with comparing the techniques and so forth.

God has proved to me over and over again that although His timing isn't mine, although His ways aren't mine, although there is no understanding the hardships faced while on this earth, the truth that He has got me in it all has finally sunk in deep enough that I can rest on that fact.

Yesterday I went out to lunch with my friend Nat, and we were talking about anything and everything. Then IVF came up, and we talked about last time, my illness with Metformin, and all that that had entailed. For a split second I forgot again that we were actually in another treatment because I have no side effects, the emotions are so different, and we've not had much contact with the clinic to make the situation seem real. I guess when scans and procedures start happening, the treatment will seem real.

Due to a power outage, the awesome Cooper family joined us for dinner, the injection time, and a great evening of hanging out. I always love spending time with dear friends, but it was extra special last night, as our champions got to see part of the process. We were also able to have an adorable toddler and baby around to remind us of the reason for all this. I can't wait! I held their baby in my arms and looked across the room at Brett, my heart filled with joy and anticipation. Oh, the day that is coming is going to be so sweet, so overwhelming, and I will surely have to pinch myself over and over again at finally having made it and being so blessed.

Getting Closer to the Big IVF Moments: March 24, 2013

Today we drew much closer to the big IVF moments, which are really exciting.

We woke and got up earlier than we usually would have on the weekend to get to Ellerslie for my blood test. Once again there were many others in the same boat, and we all sat in the waiting room, waiting for our moment to be called. My favorite lady came out and called out for "Natalia," so I started to get up from my chair, only for Natalia to be followed by a different last name. Brett and I had a little giggle about that, but the other couple were clearly too serious about the task at hand to see the funny side of it, as it's not really a common name. Anyway, before long my name was called, and I was to go to the first door on the left, and my favorite lady was once again doing the blood test; we had our usual chat about life, family, and the task at hand. Then off Brett and I went to the city for breakfast, while we waited on the scan at the public fertility clinic.

We arrived at the hospital, the parking lot being almost empty, the building not lit up like usual. A security guard checked our name off a list before permitting us to go up the elevator to the fifth floor. The clinic was quiet, with a note at reception to write our initials down and ding the bell. Before long a lovely nurse came along, named Anna, and into the room we went. As a side note, she was so lovely, and I have found my public fertility clinic version of my favorite nurse from the private fertility clinic—blessed!

We were left for me to get under the sheet, legs up in the stirrups, all ready for the doctor to come and do the scan. This time around, the monitor was moved around farther so I was able to see the follicles (a fluid-filled sac that contains an immature egg, this follicle is found in the ovary and doing the IVF drugs stimulate more), and that excited me, a visual of my miracle in waiting. The twelve follicles, ranging from six to seventeen millimeters had grown nicely, with the largest up to twenty millimeters. The endometrium (the inner lining of the uterus, which needs to be plump and ready for an embryo to nestle into and make it's home) was at twelve, which was also good.

Things were trucking along nicely, and all was looking really good. We gave each other a big high five when we were left for me to get dressed.

We went out into the corridor to wait on seeing Anna about the next steps. As we waited, I took the opportunity to once again look at the photo boards of all the miracle babies and felt such hope and anticipation at being able to have our own miracles up on the board one day. Before long Anna guided us into a consulting room to discuss details. She reiterated how happy they were; they would wait on the results from the blood, but it would likely be another night of the two injections we'd been doing: the trigger injection tomorrow and the egg collection on Wednesday. Anna sorted the extra injections needed to see that through, and we were about to head on our way. Then she looked over the notes and discussed the dummy run (where they put a catheter up into the uterus to check all will go smoothly on the day of the embryo transfer). We decided that we would leave it given how smoothly the embryo transfer's had all gone during the last IVF cycle and how easily the internal scans had happened with this round. On the day of the embryo transfer, they would do an empty catheter to just check that there were no surprises and then go with the embryo transfer.

Brett and I went on our merry way with injections in hand, another high five being had as we departed, as you need to celebrate these moments after all. We dropped by home to put the injections in the fridge and then carried on out to get a few things done. Before long Anna phoned to say the blood results were in, that it confirmed all was looking good and that we would indeed do the last injections of Buserelin and Gonal-F tonight, the trigger injection of Ovidrel tomorrow night, and the egg collection on Wednesday. Someone would phone us on Monday afternoon with the exact timing of the trigger and collection, which is all very exciting.

Then we will eagerly await the big events—how many eggs were collected, how many became embryos, how many lasted to each new day, and whether we will manage to get to a day-five embryo for transfer. Then the ultimate of the final blood test will come weeks later, the phone call to change our lives forever.

Our Egg Collection: March 27, 2013

Last night was very nice not to have to do any injections. My tender tummy from the growing follicles greatly appreciated it. We went to bed, feeling very excited for what lay ahead, so much so that I dreamed about going to the public fertility clinic. In the dream they gave us a gift, saying it was from God; it turned out to be our two miracles. I woke to realize in my excitement that I had clearly missed some relatively big steps to that.

The morning had a later start than last time, as we needed to be there at 9:45 a.m. for a 10:30 a.m. slot in theater for the egg collection. We were able to relax in bed and chat about our exciting day before getting up. I wasn't allowed breakfast with heading into theater but Brett was allowed breakfast, so he got himself sorted with that while I showered and got ready to head to the clinic. I had to try pretty hard to remember no perfume, no deodorant, and no moisturizer while I was getting dressed. I felt bare without my nail polish or jewelry too. The funny thing is, they had given instructions on not having anything scented, so the night before I had given myself a facial and asked Brett to smell my face to check that it wasn't heavily scented. Otherwise I would have had to wash it off and not put anything on. I had to laugh at the things I get my poor husband to do in the name of getting our miracles.

On the drive in, we both remarked on how much more relaxed I felt this time. It felt like we were just heading to see friends or do some errands. Last time God had been so faithful, and again it was true this time. I know this time there is a deep sense of peace, but I am sure it also had a large part to do with the fact that last time we had just found out our dear friend was on his deathbed after a long fight with cancer. That situation had caused many emotions and much anxiety, which clearly wasn't an ideal scenario to be heading into such a significant procedure.

We arrived at the clinic to find the sun shining and people bustling around the parking lot and inside the buildings. Heading up the elevator to level five, I felt my stomach flutter with excitement. We had made it to this point, and that fact filled me with such hope. I couldn't wait to find out what God had done, as I hadn't prayed about all the specifics that I had first time around. First time around I had prayed that I would get eight eggs, that four would fertilize (this is when they put the egg and sperm into a dish in the lab and it becomes an embryo) and then that the right number would last till transfer (this is where the embryo matures enough to make it viable to be transferred by a catheter into the uterus) and that at least one would be frozen (if an embryo lasts to five days it can be frozen, which is a nice safety net to have). I also prayed that I would be awake during the procedure to feel part of such a crucial moment—all of which God answered, by the way. This time, having felt so relaxed, I asked God to simply do what He felt was best on all fronts, and I looked forward to seeing how the event would unfold.

Sitting in reception, we waited for a nurse to come and get us. After some time, a new nurse we hadn't met came along, saying Anna would have been with us, but she'd gotten caught up with something else and had asked her to do the initial process. Into the recovery room we went so I could put away my bag, get into a gown, and go through the initial checks. Then the embryologist (the smart/ scientist person who puts the egg and sperm together in a dish in the lab and keeps it under a lamp and watches it develop and keeps you posted) came to discuss the steps, and Anna arrived to put in the IV and talk over a few more things. Before long the nice doctor from our first scan came along to go through her portion of it, and then we went into theater.

I hopped on the bed, legs up in stirrups, and lay back. They all went about their jobs around me. Brett sat in a chair next to me and watched all the commotion. Before long I had the blood pressure cusp on my arm, the oxygen monitor on my finger, and it was go time. Anna injected the sedatives and pain relief into the IV, which I felt very quickly. The oxygen went on, and we were set to go. I was alert and participated right from the beginning.

We all had a good banter and chat as the process went on. They were such a chilled-out and caring team, which was just perfect. They even allowed Brett to take some photos, as I wanted to share them with you guys so you could have a small peek into what the process looks like. One after one the eggs were collected, and by the end there were nine. How amazing is that. Brett and I were very happy with that result, as was the team.

From there we headed into recovery. Anna talked through some more details with us; then the embryologist once again spoke with us, and Brett took care of his portion. Thankfully I had learned from last time and had my phone handy so I wasn't bored. I texted those few who get the group updates and went on Facebook. Time passed slowly, with people coming in and out. Finally, I was discharged, and we headed out the door.

Brett and I discussed lunch, as I'd not eaten since seven thirty the night before and was feeling rather hungry. Realizing that after transfer I wouldn't be able to have sushi for nine months, we decided to go to our favorite place in Ellerslie for one last enjoyment of it. Then we went home for resting. I must admit that I'm not cramping; I don't feel the need for rest but am going to follow instructions and do my best to take it easy. There go tomorrow's plans of housework, washing, and groceries, like I usually do on a Thursday, but it's all for a good cause, so why not?

"So where to go from here?" you ask. Tomorrow the embryologist phones to let us know how many were fertilized. Then in the afternoon a nurse phones to inform us on whether the embryo transfer looks likely to be on Saturday or Monday. If there is one stand-out embryo, the transfer will go ahead on Saturday, and the nurse will give us a time on Thursday afternoon for when the embryo transfer will be, with the embryologist confirming we are good to go on Saturday morning. If a few embryos are fighting for top position (with all being around the same stage in terms of cell division and formation), then we will wait it out for Monday transfer to see which comes out on top for the best chance of success.

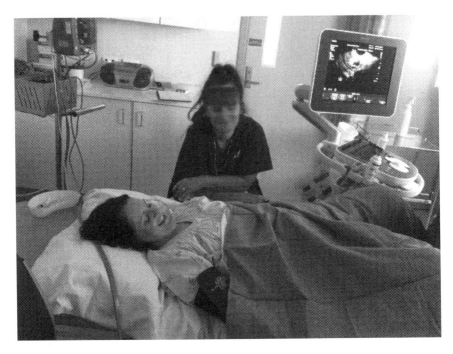

This photo is me on the theater bed taking in all the commotion around me, participating in the conversations, and feeling very blessed by God once again for allowing us to breeze through the process.

When You Meet a Bump in the Road: May 30, 2013

This morning both Brett and I woke with such excitement and anticipation at the prospect of this being the day we would get the call to confirm embryo transfer (where the embryo is taken from the dish in the lab, placed in a catheter and inserted into the uterus). With how perfectly everything was going, we expected to hear great news from the clinic on all fronts.

I couldn't help but lie in bed and think how special it was that this was all happening at Easter, such a significant time in our faith. This is the time of year when God gave life to all of us in completion and fullness. The hope bubbled deep within for this to be the final day of waking as a mum in waiting, as soon our miracle would be on board.

However, the call from the clinic came hours later. I got off the phone, feeling like we had met a bump in the road and called Brett to update him, as he was helping a friend with a new deck. Then I sent off a text to update those close friends and family: "Well, the clinic phoned, but I'm not uncontrollably grinning like expected. The transfer will go ahead today as there is one grade-two embryo (it's currently seven cells instead if eight, with one being large and will possibly divide by the time we get in to be grade one). But the other six weren't as strong as I expected to hear—three were dividing slowly, while the other three were fragmenting. She said it was possible that some of the three dividing properly would lose the fragmentation and go on to be blastocysts to be frozen, but it is hard to tell. I tried to look at it as God taking away the concern of having too many and the ethical dilemma that brings, but I was pretty disappointed. I'm hopeful for the transfer, though, and longing for this to be it, the most precious Easter ever." (For you readers who may be a little lost on the medical aspect of IVF and embryos: grade one is the best embryo you can have and has divided into eight cells, grade two is the next best and so on. A blastocyst is where the embryo has divided enough, lasted to day five and good enough to freeze and be used for a future transfer if it thaws ok. Fragmenting is where it's not divided cleanly and can affect the viability of the embryo)

When those jobs were done, I sat back, and the tears began to flow. I couldn't help it. I felt like the safety net had been ripped out from under us. I felt like we had been dealt a blow in a seemingly perfect cycle. I felt like in my human ways I was able to focus only on the negative and not on the positive. I hated that I was doubting God's gift of hope through this cycle, struggling with the fact that His ways are not mine, and fear crept in that this may not be our time after all. But how could I be feeling this way, struggling this way, when it was far from over, when there were still such good things to focus on?

The texts began to stream in from loved ones: words of hope, encouragement from God, and people seeing the positive. I appreciated the texts but also felt like, unless you've walked such a long road, you don't get that sometimes it's hard to always be strong, to always see the good, and the tears just kept flowing. It wasn't a proud moment but a real moment.

I know God will pick me up, dust me off, and carry me in His grace, but before that happens, I want to write a blog to share the reality of such a journey. It's not always glossy.

So off I went to allow God to fill me with hope once again, to get ready and head in for our transfer.

Hope Still Very Much Alive: March 31, 2013

This morning's not-so-perfect news was a surprise and really hit me. I knew while I was going through the emotions that God would graciously help me through the situation quickly. But in the same token I've shared the highs and wanted to share the lows so people walking the same path know that it's normal to have those moments. I wanted to depict the realities of such a journey.

As is often the case when I'm feeling low, the words to pray aren't always there, and I turn to singing worship songs instead. I love how God has created that desire in me, because in those moments the cloud moves away, a nearness to Him comes, and my spirits once again are lifted or are certainly on the way to being the case. After that much-needed time with God in my special armchair, I felt a lot brighter, and a nice, long hug with my man also worked wonders.

Down the hall I went to jump through the shower, and as I stood in the walk-in wardrobe to get something to wear, I realized this wasn't just any day. We would meet our miracle for the very first time, in one form at least. Somehow that knowledge made the effort seem more important, so I called Brett in to help. When I told him I needed help picking the coolest outfit because we were meeting our miracle, he smiled and obliged. He even picked a favorite T-shirt and remarked on his overly grown facial hear. I told him our baby would love him being a bear just like I did (a funny inside joke). This remark made him laugh, and he said he already loves how I'll teach the baby the funniest things to say to him.

In the car we went to the clinic, and more messages from loved ones poured in from my sad post, and those brought some emotion back. We arrived, the hospital once again like a ghost town, and made our way up in the lift. Once again we sat in reception and waited to be called. We met a new embryologist, who spoke things through with us. The embryo would be put in today, as they didn't want to risk waiting for the blastocyst stage with where things were and felt that the embryo being in its natural habitat was best for development. We learned something new, that the embryo would continue to divide inside the uterus and implant into the wall lining of the uterus only on day six. She then went over the other embryos, and once again we found out it was possible for them to carry on and for the fragmentation to sort out, but they didn't think this was overly likely.

Next the doctor came in, spoke things over, and said we would go into theater soon. A new nurse came along, and we followed her into the same room where we'd had the egg collection. Somehow the room didn't seem as fun and hopeful this time; it seemed a bit more serious. I'm not sure whether it was the change in team, whether it was the emotions of the morning or the weather outside or what. Without being able to pinpoint the issue, I quickly got on with the task at hand and was on the bed, legs in stirrups and covered with the sheet. I called out that I was ready.

The curtain was drawn, and the embryologist, doctor, and nurse were all on hand to go about their jobs. A cold gel was placed on my stomach for the ultrasound, and the not-so-glamorous side of it was completed and ready for the transfer. The catheter was being difficult, and after much prodding and pain, it was decided by the doctor that we'd take a break, so they removed the catheter. I had to smile at being told I have "interesting insides"—I told them I just like being different. An empty catheter was then tried, with the embryo safely away for when all was set for the transfer to go ahead. Thankfully it finally worked, the catheter was inplace, and then the embryo was put in to the uterus; the procedure was special to see on the screen. Then it was time to get dressed and go into the consulting room to speak with the nurse. She gave me progesterone pessaries to see us through till the blood test and talked through what needed to happen; then we went on our way.

> Here was the plan for the two-week wait:
> I was to rest for the first thirty-six hours.
> I was to take it easy till the big blood test.
> I was to have a blood test halfway to check my progesterone levels.
> I was to have the big blood test on Friday, April 12.
> There were a few others dos and don'ts included in the above.

I got home, feeling very sore from the process, and climbed into bed to rest and recover. I didn't feel the excitement and hope I had during previous times, so I wanted to shake that. I found myself starting to feel boosted as my sister and friend Hannah sent text messages of God's goodness and how He had us in this; that was just what I needed to hear. People's love and prayers carried me when I needed them, for which I am so grateful. Then my lovely friend Melva came to visit me. I spoke with my parents on Skype, and then I read an e-mail that had a Word attachment to review for another friend. I was so encouraged and uplifted, hence my saying that hope is very much alive.

That e-mail was very much God orchestrated and filled me with hope, assuring me that God is able, that He has us in this, and that it doesn't matter how things look because He is the One working miracles and doesn't need it all to be perfect to see that happen. Far from it.

Then the real treasure was a verse amid it all. Exodus 14:14 reminds us, "The Lord will fight for you; you need only to be still."

When the Going Gets Tough: April 2, 2013

There is a saying "When the going gets tough, the tough get going." That doesn't work so well for me. When the going gets tough, I turn to God.

As those of you who have followed our current IVF cycle know, everything was all going so perfectly; things were looking so promising, and in that fact it was easy to have hope and soar into confidence and expectation.

On Saturday our first blow came when we learned that six of the seven embryos weren't progressing as hoped, but there was still a possibility of having some make it to have as a backup. The second blow came today when the lovely embryologist phoned to say that none had made it to blastocyst stage and that there were none to freeze, as they were all of poor quality. She told me that given that I wanted any that hadn't made it to be returned rather than discarded, they would be ready for me to collect if I could just let them know when.

I hung up the phone, feeling like I had received a blow to my stomach. I was stunned. This news wasn't what I had been expecting. I felt sad. I touched my stomach, wondering whether the embryo inside was also of poor quality or whether there had been the continued cell division needed for implantation today. I phoned Brett, but the words wouldn't come out. Seconds passed, but it felt like longer. I told him that none had made it. I cried. He was brave; he was strong. He told me that all we needed was this one on board, and we had to focus on that. The tears flowed, and I told him I didn't want to go through this experience again; the process had been too long and hard. I just needed this to be our time. There was nothing left to be said, as all we could do was give the matter to God and wait. I asked whether he could please let those we had been texting have updates to know what had happened, as I couldn't face the responses. Then I got off the phone and just stared ahead, thoughts racing, tears flowing.

I asked God to please allow this embryo to have divided and to be nestling in my womb, for this to be our moment. I asked for this to be life within as I rested my hand on my stomach, longing for Him to grant this as our time. There was a battle, and I wanted it won. I told Him that I didn't have much left in me and that all I could do was give it to Him, knowing He knew my heart's cry and that those supporting us would pray all the right things when I couldn't.

Then I felt numb, so I kept on with some business paper work. I looked at the time, knowing it wouldn't be long till Nat would turn up for our planned catch-up. I had picked up my phone many times to suggest we leave it for another day, as I wasn't really feeling in the mood. But each time I put the phone down, thinking it would be better for me to have our catch-up. There was a knock on the door, and she was there, with her baby in hand. I knew from her smiling face that she hadn't yet heard the news, and we had a normal catch-up for the first half.

Finally, I decided I should tell her the news, which ended with both of us in tears. She said she didn't know how people without faith could walk this journey, saying that because I trusted in God and His plan, no matter what, we would be ok. As she doesn't have that relationship with God, her words meant even more, and I couldn't agree more.

Once she left, I wondered what to do with my day; I could do many things, but I was also supposed to take it easy, so trying to find that balance wasn't easy. I phoned my babe again to see how he was doing, as the news had sunk in, also wanting to assure him that there was bounce back in my step, even if just a little. We love each other deeply, and I know that if he hears I'm okay, that helps him to be okay too. So I wanted to ensure that happened. It is always nice to hear his voice and to be able to chat about hard or fun things.

The song "How Great Is Our God" by Chris Tomlin came to mind, and soon I pushed play, and the music engulfed me as I sat on the couch, tears streaming once again. I knew that no matter how our circumstances seem, God is in control, and His ways are greater. I know that He has given us a promise for our babies, and when it happens, people will see that our God is faithful, that His ways are perfect. The lyrics seem so very fitting.

We still have a week and a half of waiting before the big blood test. This is far from over, and there is still every reason to have hope, for that to remain the theme of this cycle. Thankfully each day between now and then, I have a fun activity planned. Next week will be the ultimate—with my waiting party (a time to celebrate hope and friendship with some of my closest and dearest girlfriends), with speaking at Carey College about the book, with a MAC makeup session, with my Bible study, and with the big blood test.

I'm sure that in that time, there will be emotions, and this journey will continue to bring highs and lows as we wait it out. But I'm keeping my trust and focus on God. I am putting my hope in Him alone and waiting for the day when people can celebrate this miracle with us and see how great my God truly is.

It would be so easy to crumble when we are given those blows, to hold out on God in frustration, but when the going gets tough, I will still turn to Him—in fact, even more. No matter what, I will still lift His name high and sing worship songs while I walk the highs and lows of life. God is where my hope, strength, and ability to keep on comes from. Without Him, who knows where I'd be?

Thankful: April 5, 2013

Yesterday would have been my usual housework day. I know many people would love the excuse to leave it, but for me I find such joy in cleaning my house and consider it "me time." I love cranking my worship music and just being in my own space. I woke, knowing I should be resting and couldn't do this. My limitation make me feel frustrated. I was getting very bored. Resting isn't a natural inclination of mine.

The lack of activity gave my mind time to be consumed with many things. I began to question whether those untruths people had said had any weight. Would this really not happen if I struggled with hope and fear, if I had doubts and felt sad due to my situation? Were people right that there was something I had done or not dealt with that put a roadblock between us and having a family? I hated that these thoughts were happening, and I didn't know what to do with my time and my overthinking and analyzing ways.

As the afternoon drew on, I let go of the frustration. I enjoyed being on the couch and watching YouTube clips of my favorite worship music. I looked online at possibilities for the nursery. I looked through photos of an amazing ten years with my man and thought about how blessed I am. My thoughts and perspectives flipped around.

This morning I again brought up a song by Chris Tomlin called "Amazing Grace—My Chains Are Gone" and thought about its lyrics. You see, when I was sixteen, I started praying for my to-be husband. I prayed such specifics because of the abuse that had happened in my past and the need for a man I thought couldn't possibly exist—someone to love me unconditionally, someone to protect and care for me, someone to invest in the marriage as much as I did—and the list went on. When I was eighteen, a guest speaker told me that God had a man for me who was so special that I didn't need to fear marriage, that I would be adored and loved like I had never known, that he would never let me down (I was scared of this). Then a year later, Brett and I started going out, and to this day I'm blown away because of how accurate those words were, how blessed I am, and how God has gifted me with a husband who continually astounds me.

My thoughts turned to our desire for a family, to the promises I believe God has given us for a family (in short in 2005 I cried out to God on two occasions for answers and clarity, and both times He used a woman we didn't know to speak to me confirming we would have babies, they would be conceived by us, there were no hoops we could jump through to make it happen, to wait on God's timing), and to the two-week wait we were currently in. I know Brett feels like he is holding his breath as we wait, that he wants to protect us from more hurt, and I am trying to be as full of hope as I can possibly be, because I can't face the thought of this round of IVF failing. When I think of those two coping mechanisms (worship music and reflecting on what God has promised and where He's been faithful on other promises to give confidence for the one yet to be realized) and then ponder the lyrics, I can't help but think that God really does have us in this situation, more than I could possibly realize, just as He had me way back in my teen years when it came to God's promise of a marriage, Brett coming along and all we share. "The Lord has promised good to me," and I am so very thankful for that.

Then I opened up my devotional, and what do you know but the title was "When Doubt Creeps In." It went on to give these gems:

- All things are possible to him who believes (Mark 9:23).
- Doubt isn't a sin; it's sin only if it translates into rejecting God.
- To be human is to sometimes doubt, even the most basic elements of our faith. In fact, doubt can be an instrument for building faith.
- Psalm 94:19 is a tender reminder of God's love for the doubter: "When doubts filled my mind, your comfort gave me renewed hope and cheer."[2]

I'm so thankful for how God brings about encouragement and words in the time frames I need. I'm so thankful that God has given me such blessings, and because of what He has done, I know there is so much reason to hope for what will be.

When It Becomes Hour by Hour: April 8, 2013

It was only yesterday that Brett and I discussed the week ahead and that each new day would be a milestone to making it to Friday— the day of the big tell-all blood test.

How quickly things can change … Last night I had some spotting, and this morning I woke, nervously wondering what the day would hold and what my body was doing.

It was meant to be a day full of fun, as it was my waiting party with dear friends. We would celebrate hope and friendship, and enjoy company and food. A month earlier, I had excitedly ordered cupcakes from the talented Annalise, made up the menu I wanted, written thank-you notes, and purchased little party favors of Orly nail polish and hand creams. It was meant to be a time to make them feel special and just have a lot of fun together.

As I got into the shower and saw more than the previous spotting, my body crumpled, the tears streamed down my face. All I could muster was "No, no, no" as I looked to the heavens. This needed to be our time; that was all there was to it. I wouldn't accept the day going like other times had. No!

I phoned Brett, saying I didn't want to be phoning, nor did I feel I shouldn't tell him first when I was about to phone the clinic, as they had instructed if there was bleeding. There was such heaviness in that phone conversation. I phoned the clinic at eight thirty and was only able to leave a message and wait, a painfully long wait.

I looked at the clock, and there was only an hour and a half before people would arrive for the party. I had set up earlier, and it was just a matter of people turning up and getting a few final things from the fridge. I didn't know what to do with myself, as this sadness, despair, and anxiety engulfed me. I found myself sitting in my chair, the sun streaming in and the sobs welling up from deep within. All I could do was turn to God and cry out to Him to sustain us no matter what lay ahead, to work a miracle and still allow this to be our time, to help me to still go on with this party.

I messaged my sister, as I felt I needed added prayers to mine. She was unable to make it to the party, so it didn't matter whether she knew, but I didn't want anyone else who was coming to know. I didn't want there to be sadness when the event was meant to be one of joy and celebration for how special they are and how much I appreciate their walking this journey with me. As I sobbed and the words came, she suggested texting everyone to say the party was off. The advice was wise, I know, but people had altered plans and were driving from afar, so I didn't want to do that. I always stick to my commitments.

Hannah arrived early from Cambridge to see a puffy face from tears, so I filled her in but asked her to keep the news to herself, as I didn't want to ruin the party. She respected that and talked as I put on some makeup to hide the current realities. The door knocks began, and my dear friends and their kids poured into my home. There was chatting, food was enjoyed, kids played, and there was much activity. I did my best to participate, to make the event about them and not to ruin it.

At one point, I went off to the toilet, and after seeing there had been no further bleeding, I got the phone and whispered an update to Brett before heading back to the party. I was still nervous and waited for the call from the clinic. The hours passed, and once again I was alone in the house. The next anxious trip to the toilet showed slight spotting, and I once again updated Brett and tried the clinic again.

At last the clinic phoned and said that there was nothing I could do, more than I already had, to prevent a period from coming if it was on its way. It was too early to have a blood test or scan; I needed to simply wait it out and take it hour by hour. If things progressed with bleeding, I was to give them a call; otherwise they wished all the best with it stopping and my making it to Friday.

I have heard countless stories of others having spotting and even bleeding and still getting their "happy ever after." I'm hopeful and know we are still in with a chance, but there is also that part of me that has walked this road for too many years to be so naïve as to know how it can also turn out another way.

So here we are … taking it hour by hour, once again leaning on God to carry us and thankful that even in this He holds us and is a good God. I'm grateful for a love so deep with my man that it will see me through all trials and triumphs. I appreciate the fact that I have friends who are there for me—hoping, praying, and caring through whatever lies ahead.

The Doors God Opens: April 9, 2013

I love how God works. Back in December last year, I was asked to speak at Carey Baptist College about the book and our journey. The invitation actually made me laugh. Really, people, me? But I had told God when the book launched that, despite how scared I might be, if He opened doors, I would say yes. The time was set for April 9, and with the event being months off, I pushed it out of my mind.

Before I knew it, that day came. You would think it's not ideal timing to speak to a room full of strangers about a journey as emotional as infertility when one is going through IVF, but to top it off, I had started spotting too. People questioned whether I should bail, but the clinic had said it would be fine, and I had made a commitment, and I was going to honor that and be obedient to God.

The organizer of this had kindly asked whether there were any off-limit questions since it is such a sensitive topic. They arranged a lady to meet me at reception and give me a run-through of what to expect. I felt somewhat prepared and in the know because of this. On the way I didn't feel nervous, as I figured it was on God and not on me to pull this off, so I just asked that He would indeed give me the strength not to be a teary mess and manage to share something.

I arrived, and a lovely lady greeted me and guided me over to the right area. They were finishing chapel and then would head to the dining hall. Before long I was sitting at a table, eating lunch, and having a chat with a few people; then it was time for me to speak. I stepped onto the small stage, picked up the microphone, and leaned on the stool (I'm far too short to climb up on such a tall stool and stay there). I was ready to have questions asked of me.

There were moments when I welled up with tears, but I didn't even need the tissue cleverly tucked in my pocket for the time I had anticipated. There were no nerves as I spoke about something so private and heartbreaking, looking around the room and making eye contact where I could. God once again had me in this and took care of it all as I needed. Phew! Afterward the floor was opened to questions, and people later came up to chat. I was blown away by how caring everyone was, how much people could relate, and the lovely words they said. I came away feeling blessed.

I love how God can use ordinary people like me to share with others about a journey that is all too often swept under the carpet. Even though I'm still walking this journey and have my own heartache, I love how God has given me a heart for people, a desire to share and help where I can. I love how He opens doors for me to do that and how He blesses me through it too. It certainly isn't my strength or ability; it is once again all Him and His provision.

Then I went home to the reality of the increased spotting, but still I could smile because God has got us, even in this. I opened up the computer to share about today, and there was a message from a stranger with just the right encouragement needed.

No Go Yet Again: April 12, 2013

Once again the moment came to have the all-telling blood test, only to be told once again that it was a no go. Today marks us having walked this journey for *eight years, seven months, two weeks, and three days*. I don't understand why a cycle that seemed to have the theme of hope has ended in such a sad way. I don't understand why the promises I believe we have been given for our babies is still unobtainable to date. I don't understand what more could possibly be expected of us, and I don't know what is ahead. I feel such heartache, sadness, and confusion in this moment. I'm trying desperately to hold onto some shred of hope, to figure out God's plan, and to be able to carry on.

Making a Choice: April 18, 2013

The week leading up to the blood test was filled with so many emotions—on the one hand, there was hope for a miracle despite the spotting, but there were also tears as I processed what seemed to be inevitable once again.

Friday morning came, and I woke with a certainty in my inner being that this too wasn't our time—so much so that I drafted a blog so people weren't left hanging, but I didn't need to take time out later when all I wanted was time with my babe. I went about my morning routine and headed to have the blood test taken. Surrounding me were pregnant women tenderly touching their rounded bellies and asking for drinks of water. I looked at my phone, trying to fight the tears. *Really, people. Today you need to show off your bumps?*

I drove to my Bible study, wondering just how the day would play out. Would I once again find myself in a puddle of tears, feeling angry with God that His timing wasn't mine yet again? Would I struggle to have hope? Would we cope with another blow and whatever was ahead?

Walking into the church, I slipped in, as the singing had already started. The words were so fitting for such a day, and a peace and strength washed over me. God's promise to me earlier in the year, that He would have us in this and that it wasn't up to me to pick myself up and move forward, was so encouraging, and I could certainly see this truth being played out.

Reaching home just after lunchtime, I was grateful that Brett would be home any minute. We decided that after the clock watching last time, we would go out and get a new dining room suite sorted instead. As we pulled up to the shop for the chairs, the phone rang, and it was the lovely nurse from the public fertility clinic. I could hear in her voice that it wasn't good news, as expected. Once again we went through the process of being told it was a no go, of someone feeling sorry for us, of discussing where to go from here, and of finding out that our second round of public IVF would be in September. I think the previous day's tears and processing allowed us to once again deal with the news relatively well.

Brett and I held hands, looked at each other, and agreed to head into the shop anyway. Once we came out of there, I texted family and friends to let them know it was a no go once again. As we drove to the next place to purchase the timber for Brett to make the table, the texts came flooding in, and my eyes welled up with tears with all the words being said. Once again outside the next place, we shared a moment and went in to make the decision for the table.

As I sat in reception, the texts continued streaming in. I knew, from what people were saying and what we had done in the past, that we could cocoon ourselves and process this blow, wallowing in the current reality; or we could trust in God, continue to take steps of faith, and live life. Brett came back in from the yard, and I asked whether he was up to going out for dinner with friends, as I didn't want to wallow in self-pity at home for the night. Thankfully I married a like-minded man, and plans were set in motion.

We had a lovely evening with friends, and as we left Mexico in Takapuna, I suggested that we go to Albany, a suburb close by that had a big mall, as I was certain it would still be open. That week a Peter Alexander catalog had arrived in the mail, and there had been a pair of girls' pj's with ducks on them. I had thought it would be a cool gift as a celebration, but as the week wore on, I realized that wouldn't be the case. Instead it was a purchase of hope. Sure, we had just been dealt a blow, but I had faith that God's promises would still come to fruition; I just didn't know when. This felt like a tangible way of holding onto hope as we pressed forward yet again.

On the weekend we were busy with working on a friend's property, as arranged, looking at sections (which some of you would call bare land, or a block) that had come up for sale (in the hopes of starting the building process yet again) as well as spending some much-needed one-on-one time with each other. Then we were into the swing of yet another week, with doing business paper work and getting jobs done around the house (that had been put off while I was taking it easy with the IVF process) and some errands.

I decided that on Monday it was best to do all my Bible study homework to start my week off on the right footing and then move onto the jobs. I was so grateful to be able to sink myself into that, to focus on the goodness of God and the promises He has given and the assurances needed.

Yesterday I had arranged to pick up the six failed embryos to join the previous two failed embryos in the pot we had a red rose. As

I got ready, there was once again that hit of sadness because of the realities of such a journey and the significance of what I was doing. I arrived at the hospital to see many pregnant ladies walking around the ground floor; then I went up in the lift to the clinic; a couple with an adorable little baby girl greeted me. As I sat in reception, I pondered how cruel seeing their baby girl felt, but none of them could have known what impact their situation had on me at such a moment. This is just life. Again I was faced with a choice—to have a pity party over what I didn't have and longed for or to be thankful for what I *did* have and be expectant for what lay ahead.

A number of people have asked questions over the past week:

- How can I still have hope when we have been dealt so many blows?
- How can I keep getting up and moving forward time after time?
- How can I still think God is faithful and good when I'm going through more disappointment?

Well, the answer is simple really—life is about perspective, it's about choices, and it's about God.

I believe with all my heart that over the years we have been given words, promises, and encouragement that we will have our babies, so those enable me to keep going and to have hope for that day.

I have grown in my understanding of myself and God through my hardest time and brokenness in 2011. They have given me a foundation that enables me to trust in Him and see things in a new way.

God truly has carried us in the ups and downs in small and big ways. He's given us each other, He's given us words of encouragement when needed, and He's allowed us to cope with the physical and emotional parts of such a journey. The strength is truly from Him and not from me. People give me far too much credit for what they perceive as me being hopeful, positive, strong, brave—as me having a high pain tolerance—and so forth. I'm simply leaning on God, and He is doing the rest.

Even When We Can't See It, God Knows Best: May 6, 2013

Today a dear friend of mine had to put drops in to her daughter's eyes; both of them had to be brave. Her little girl was understandably not a fan of the drops, and my friend found it hard to put her precious girl through that process but knew it was for her good, so they had to be brave and persist with it.

This story got me thinking, and I pondered how it gave me a small glimmer into what it must be like for God sometimes. No doubt it must pain Him to see us go through the valleys of life, but at the same time, He knows the full picture and sees that in the long term, the trial is for the best. As I thought over this matter, my morning devotional came to mind, as did my previous Bible study homework. All came in the same light of God carrying us through the hardships and promising good to us. There is a choice in that moment of hardship to choose to walk it with God or to push Him away and throw a good old "tanty" (or tantrum to most, which I have done a few times, I might add). I've got to say that walking this road with God is far better.

Even when we can't always see, even when we're in the depths of the valley and longing for the light at the end, God really does know best. One day when we can see the full picture, we will be grateful for His perseverance when it no doubt broke His heart.

Don't get me wrong; this doesn't mean the trial won't be hard. This doesn't mean we can't cry and feel all the emotions we need to process at such a time. I'm just sharing something that came to mind through a friend's experience and hope it will encourage you as it did me.

When Empathy Comes from a Place of Pain: May 19, 2013

I have lived with painful periods since age eleven, and somehow that break with Zoladex and IVF made the blow of this round of pain difficult. My limitations frustrated me. I was unwilling to accept that this was my lot, and there was a real weariness in the journey walked.

The week wore on, and a few significant events happened that made me reflect on things as I lay in bed with pain-killers by my bedside, heat packs at the ready, and the laptop at my fingertips as I tried to express what was on my mind.

Through the paths I've crossed in our infertility journey, I've come to know a friend of a friend, who is currently going through her first round of IVF. You can read about what people go through; you can join support groups and try your best to prepare yourself on every level. But until you start it, you can't comprehend what it's like, and nothing can prepare you for the physical and emotional side of it all, let alone the unspoken aspects, even in support groups. I woke at four o'clock on Friday morning with her heavily on my heart, so I prayed, and still she weighed heavily on my heart, so I sent her an e-mail. I got a response, and she was so grateful that God was using my empathy to support her, as she was struggling.

Friday was my day for the Bible study, but I was tired, and the pain intensified to that level that I writhed in pain, not knowing what to do with myself. However, the study had been such a great one that week, and I didn't want to miss out on the gems I knew I would glean if I went. So off I went, and as I sat there in my small group, intense pain seared through my body, and I struggled to concentrate. Someone asked me a question, and reading what was on my page took all my strength. An interruption happened, and my gaze left the page for a moment. I looked back at the page to keep on as asked, and the words were a blur, the pain simply unbearable. The heat felt like I was going to combust, and this was when I handed the page to the woman beside me, muttering that the pain was too intense. Could she read it, please? Her voice was muffled. I could feel the sympathetic looks, and in that moment they became too much.

The tears spilled over, and there came a deep sob from within. I was embarrassed that I didn't have the strength to hold myself together. I was angry with myself for the limitations and reality of this world of pain I had to endure. I wished that I wasn't so stubborn and had just stayed at home.

This morning the lady going through her first round of IVF e-mailed her support people, saying how things were going and what was ahead. Due to circumstances, she would have her first scan on her own, and my heart went out to her. My first instinct was to offer to be there for her if she wanted. I knew the cost it would be for me with my pain levels, it had already been a crazy week, and I knew the emotion it would hold, but still I wanted to go. So I offered, she accepted, and I locked the event in my calendar. I know God will give me all I need to be with her in the moment.

My mind wandered to her saying how blessed she was that God was using my empathy in the way He was, since many don't allow their journeys to be used for others or go out of their way to support others. I googled the word *empathy* vs. sympathy and found this: "Empathy: Understanding what others are feeling because you have experienced it yourself or can put yourself in their shoes. Sympathy: Acknowledging another person's emotional hardships and providing comfort and assurance."

I thought back to a moment in my youth, when a guest speaker at church had said the painful journey I walked would be used to walk beside others and have an impact in their lives. I naïvely thought at the time that it would be from my history of sexual abuse. In this past year, I see that the painful journey mentioned way back then hadn't even been; it is this journey of infertility we are still on. Then just recently my old youth group leader shared that in their Bible study in the States they were studying about faith and how some people can use their time of valleys to grow, change, and help others or simply waste their opportunities.

As I think on all that, I don't want to bolster myself up at all, because my flaws are many, and there is a book that shows my struggles, insecurities, and flaws. I can't very well pretend otherwise now. But what it did make me realize is how far God has brought me and changed me, how blessed I am with a God who can use my broken self and a husband who loves me unconditionally regardless of that, and how even when I feel otherwise, I am useful.

All too often we want life to be easy; we want perfection; and the society around us only inflames that. Will you allow a true empathy to come from the place of pain? Will you allow God to create growth and change in the valley? Will you allow people to see the imperfect parts of your life? The journey sure isn't easy, but it sure is worth it.

Wading Through: May 21, 2013

There are very few times now when I will have that negative whisper in my ear about how I'm useless, because I'm not good for much when experiencing a lot of pain; or about how I'm inadequate as a wife, because I can't even produce children. I ignore that whisper about how much of a drain I am on my friends, because I'm still struggling with this journey of infertility; or about how God isn't going to come through with my miracle babies, and I'll have egg on my face for having hung on for so long.

This weekend those negative whispers tried their hardest to be heard, and with my lack of sleep, physical pain, and hurting heart, they began to penetrate deeper. I began to feel like such a failure, and I could certainly not see what others said about my strength or faith. I woke this morning, feeling rather deflated, and am so very grateful for being able to sit at my desk with my heat packs, do my Bible study homework, and have those negative voices turn to shreds.

We are studying Genesis at the moment. In fact, we are in chapters 12 and 13, where Abraham is introduced, known as a man of faith. For those not in the know, he was a man to whom God promised offspring, but he was very old, and his wife was old and barren to boot. The promise was amazing, let alone his believing and the promise coming to pass.

As I read over the notes and started reading the Bible and answering the questions, I felt overwhelmed that God was yet again so faithful to me and that this study was so timely for where I was. I could be boosted in the journey yet again as I pored over the homework and found these gems:

– When God didn't keep His promise quickly enough, Abraham tried self-effort along with cultural convention to fulfill God's plan. Finally, Abraham understood that impossible situations are opportunities to trust God and prove His powers. He believed God's promise, even though he couldn't see how God would accomplish it. God created life within Sarah and Abraham's aged bodies, and miraculously Isaac was born.
– Though Abraham didn't understand, he trusted God and obeyed one step at a time. Will you, like Abraham, pursue God's place or path for you? You will find that God gives you much more than all you may seem to lose.
– Romans 10:11 says, "Anyone who trusts in Him will never be put to shame."
– In the homework there was a question about how we had experienced God's faithfulness as Abraham had. I actually had to come back to the answer at the end of the section, because it was amazing for me to think over and realize how much He has blessed me and how faithful He has been in all the peaks and valleys of life. The song by New Breed "Oh How He Loves Us" came to mind, and I felt so thankful that I was able to do this study and wade through the negative whispers to the truths.

It's encouraging to know that even a godly man who was known in the Bible as a great man of faith had his moments. That makes it okay for me to wade through this road we find ourselves on.

Living, Not Merely Surviving: May 24, 2013

Last night Brett and I went to the Hollie Smith concert, and her closing song was "Bathe in the river". The people around us were drinking their wine and having a chat, and through the clutter of it all, I immersed myself in the soulful music and the lyrics. The song really resonated with me. As the last notes played, I reflected on my day, on how far we have come in our journey, and on what lies ahead.

That very morning I had woken early to support a special lady at her first IVF scan. I was nervous as I backed out of the drive. I didn't know her as well as one would expect for such a vulnerable moment. I wasn't sure whether the lighthearted and hopeful approach Brett and I adopt in these situations was what she would want or need. If it wasn't, what would she need, and how would I gauge it? I wasn't sure how I would feel going back to the clinic, especially with it being a week of such physical pain and since I was so tired.

I put my worship music on and started to pray. By the time I arrived, I had an excitement in my being at the privilege of being able to support her through all the doors God has opened in our journey. I felt confident that I would be able to gauge what she needed and would simply go in with my normal manner to start with and see how it played out. As I parked the car and started the walk to the lift, the hospital felt so familiar, and I don't really know how one could feel this way about a fertility clinic, but it felt comfortable like it had become my stamping ground. There was such a peace in being back.

This special lady did exceptionally well, and I'm really proud of how well she did. I'm so excited for the positive results for this first stage and so pleased she was able to have the incredible nurse Anna with her in that moment. I left feeling so blessed, and as I drove away, how fitting it was to see a brilliant rainbow in the sky. It reminded me that God's faithfulness is new every morning.

I then went to my training day for a new product range used at my home beauty business. The lady who presents is so lovely. The last time I had been to a training day on products was when the book was in its final stages to be launched, so she asked about it, and I was able to fill her in. She remarked on how well I looked and said there was a real difference since last time. As the training continued, another lady said how many woman going through IVF had come to her for treatments and their skin needs. Being able to share from experience, I made suggestions. At the end she wanted to share about a miracle her neighbor had experienced after a long journey. She then said what a difference "relaxing" can make. I smiled and was gracious about all that comes with the "relax and it will happen" comments.

As I drove home, my mind ticked over all that had been said, and I realized how cathartic the launch of *A Mum in Waiting* had been for me. I was really able to close that chapter and live in this next one. Yes, there are still treatments and still heartaches and emotions. But I don't feel like I'm treading water to survive. I feel like I'm truly living and enjoying all God is blessing us with. Over the past six months, God has done such life-altering work in me to bring healing, wholeness, and a deep hope as we continue on. How very fitting it was to finish the day reflecting on the lyrics of that song (mentioned above).

Wearing the Wrong Pants: June 10, 2013

I seem to have my grumpy and sad pants on, and I gotta say, I'm not loving it. There are many things that have brought me to wear the wrong pants, and they've all added up to not being such a fun time as I process it all and try to get on the right side again.

- My endometriosis pain has been back in full force, which has made me feel very tired and weary of living with pain. But because I long for our miracles, I'm stuck between a rock and a hard place when it comes to resolving it.
- I'm over the comments that are flooding in on how lucky we are to be a couple and have time to do what we like or "just wait till it's your turn, and you see what we mean." Really! I long for the day when I'm a parent, not slogging my guts out

to get to it. So my perspective is very different compared to theirs, making the comments a little hard to swallow.

- My nephew is turning nine this weekend, and while I adore him and love seeing him grow and reach all his milestones, the birthday is also a little hard. It marks how long we have been on this journey.

He was born in June 2004, and rushing down to Hamilton to meet him was so precious. I will never forget walking into the room and seeing this amazing little baby in a cute, little, yellow all-in-one lying on the bed and having my first hold. I was smitten, and it was wonderful to be an auntie.

Brett and I walked out into the brisk air, and although we had already been talking about when I would come off the pill to start a family, that night we were even more excited about what lay ahead, and nothing could compare to that moment.

With my nephew now turning nine, his birthday reminds me of how the nine-year mark of our journey is fast approaching. This reminds me that if all had gone according to plan, we would have been the parents of an eight-year-old and a six-year-old. It's not till you get that picture that you realize how truly long this journey is and how different life would be.

While I see God's hand on our lives and know what we have gained through the pain, that fact doesn't soften the blow right now.

On a timely weekend, a package arrived from my parents, who live in Indonesia. My mum was out shopping with a friend for her grandchildren when she spotted these two duck all-in-ones. She couldn't help herself and made the purchase, to be added with our other precious items as we continue to walk this journey in hope. That was perfectly timed encouragement as we keep on in hope.

I can't help but wonder, though. How much longer? What more is ahead? How much more are we to endure? Will I be able to be the mum I hope to stack up to when the moment finally comes?

I for one am praying that we get a double miracle and that the timing will be sooner rather than later so we can graduate from this journey and finally be a family of four.

Letting It Sink In: June 17, 2013

Sometimes when God opens and closes doors, I don't entirely get it. I can't see the big picture, and His plan doesn't make a whole lot of sense to me. But as time goes by, some pieces of the puzzles become clearer. This year seems to be a real mix of just that for me.

I've had the privilege of meeting a number of lovely ladies who are in various stages of their own journeys through the book and this blog, as they've reached out. As I've listened to them share, answered some of their questions, and been able to walk beside them where needed, I've seen that the road I've walked has meaning for others.

On the day our IVF cycle in April failed, we found the very place we had been looking for, a place to build a family home and settle in for many years to come. The way the plan unfolded was amazing to see, and you could see God's hand all over it. I'm excited as we go through the building process and anticipate what is ahead. The land for our home helps me feel more okay with the disappointment of April and to trust in Him as we keep on.

This year, as I've studied Genesis in my Bible study, I've seen God work in my life with the residual anger and hurt I'd been holding onto from the actions of others in our darkest moments. I've seen my extreme need to have control or have my home just so melt away. My character is being fine-tuned on a deeper level in many regards.

I never wanted to be involved in leadership; I didn't want to be in the limelight and just wanted a simple and comfortable life. I would resist when people said they saw God using me on a bigger scale. When I thought about our family having an impact, I always thought on a very small scale. I was stubborn and took a lot of time to battle it out, overthink it, and doubt myself before saying yes to where I felt God was leading me. Last year, with the launch of the book, I was taken very far from my comfort zone, and I thought surely it would stop there. But I was silly enough to tell God that, with the start of this year, I would follow wherever He led; and I've seen that quick obedience happen time and time again, all well outside my comfort zone.

Once again God is taking me well outside my comfort zone. I was asked to be a children's leader at my Bible study a few weeks back. The opportunity was out of left field for me and didn't fit in with what I saw my year being, and yet within minutes of being asked, I knew my answer should be yes. That didn't stop all my doubts and fears, though. I wondered when God and the team would realize they had the wrong person. I was scared that I would turn up and that none of the kids would like me, therefore making me feel insecure about having my own kids and questioning whether doing this and inevitably loving these kids would mean that the dream for our own family would be altered. And the list went on and on. But here goes, with it starting this week. I'll see how it all unfolds.

The road we map out for ourselves is rarely ever what ends up being God's map for our lives. But even in the hardest of times, even in the strangest of routes, I can see the richness of God's road and how much greater it is than my own. I'm finally letting that truth sink in deeper.

How about you? Can you see God's hand on your life, whether it's the road you expected or one far from it? Can you look beyond the hardships to see the fullness and richness? I hope so.

Defying All Logic: July 11, 2013

This morning I saw my husband off at the door, walked in, and picked up my devotional, nestling into the chair. Once I was finished, I looked up and saw the new piece of hope I had on the wall (a paper-tole Minnie and Mickey in frames) and realized there is such a joy and peace within, which defies all logic.

When I look back over the brokenness, heartache, torturous health, and struggles of 2011 and 2012, the enormity of God's grace and provision to get to where I am in this year blows me away.

The realization of that progress led me to open the cupboard door, pull down the box of treasures, and look through the purchases of hope to mark many milestones in this almost-nine-year journey. Excitement and anticipation welled up within as I looked forward to the day when these weren't mere treasures in a box to hold onto hope but were to be used and enjoyed when our miracles arrived. The very thought brought an even greater joy, deeper hope, and a peace that passes all understanding. I'm so grateful that God has put the fragmented pieces back together, that He has brought healing in all forms of the word, and that this year is so very different.

Next month will be the nine-year milestone for us, and once again, defying all odds, there isn't that anxious dread, that gut-wrenching heartache as the moment looms—well, in this moment anyway. In the past few months, I have seen the hand of God at work in a way that blows my mind and leaves me overwhelmed and so very grateful. I may not know when the day for our miracle is coming. I may not know what is ahead in all aspects, but what I do know is that if things had gone according to my way and timing, there are so many blessings and growth I would have missed out on. In *all* things, there is every reason to have hope, joy, and peace.

Once Upon a Time: August 1, 2013

Brett and I married well over ten years ago now. On our big day, his uncle recorded the various moments for us, and back then it was on VHS. For years I'd thought about getting it converted from VHS to DVD so we had it on record for years to come; I'd just never gotten around to it. Well, this year I finally made it happen, and on Monday the courier dropped off the result.

We sat down with our dinner, all excited to watch the DVD, reminisce, see special faces, and enjoy it. It started with the bridesmaids and I getting ready at my parents' house, and Brett remarked on how much younger I looked. Soon after that, he said, "If only we could warn her what was ahead." In the shot were me; a family member, who had gone through great heartache; and my bridesmaid, who lost her husband to cancer last year. I had thought he was talking about one of them, but he meant me. I reflected on that thought and am grateful we were blissfully unaware of what lay ahead so we could enjoy each moment as it came and deal with the hardships as needed.

The moment of reflection quickly passed, as the fun of getting into the dress and heading to the church happened before my eyes. Oh, the anticipation, excitement, and happiness I felt at that moment. Before I knew it, we watched me walking down the aisle, and I once again felt the emotion of that day. I looked over at my babe, and you could see he too was reliving that wonderful and overwhelming moment.

I loved watching the wedding, seeing that absolute love and delight on our faces, getting glimpses of the special people in our lives, laughing at the speeches, and reliving the magical and life-changing day. But what got me most of all was the encouragement I found in watching it. You see, three significant things showed me that even back then, God had us, even though we didn't know what was ahead. He did and was paving the way for us to be able not only to endure it but also to grow through it and capture the good.

The first moment of encouragement was when our friend, who was speaking before the vows, shared the Bible story of how a wife was found for Isaac. He went into how the servant found Rebekah, someone who went above and beyond. He said that we were two people who went above and beyond, but we needed to apply that quality to our marriage too. It's amazing to see how that has played out (even when, truth be told, I wasn't listening to a word being said during his talk on that day because I was too caught up in other things). God brought the best person possible to be beside me in life, and I am so thankful that we both go above and beyond for each other; it's the reason we have a marriage and friendship like we do.

The next moment came from my dear friend, who wrote and sang a song during the signing of the register. The key words that stuck out to me, as tears slid down my check, were about a love that was everlasting and a friendship that was the best of friends and enduring. I felt overwhelmed by how those words have reflected a husband and best friend who has cared for me in ways I couldn't have ever imagined or hoped for, given all we have gone through with this journey. Once again I'm blessed to see the hand of God and the provision in the man I'm fortunate to call my husband and best friend.

The final moment was during the speeches, when my dad shared the moment when Brett and I turned from being friends to going out. Then his mum responded in her speech about how this change had played out in her household. You see, Brett and I had been friends for a long time, and sadly my just wanting to be friends when I'd previously learned of his feelings had burned him, so he was playing it safe. The friendship blossomed into more on both sides this time around. We hung out, we e-mailed, and I agonized over how he felt and what I should do. Finally, one day when I was responding to an e-mail, I decided to convey my feelings beyond friendship among the other words; there was a chance that Brett would skip over my words if the feeling wasn't reciprocated.

Once the e-mail was written, I came out to the kitchen and agonized over the decision and words once again by telling my mum and asking for direction. She obviously wasn't much help, as I said I would pray about the matter and headed off. I then came out and said I had sent it; I had prayed that if the relationship was meant to be, he would receive my words on his end. And if the relationship wasn't meant to be, my words would get lost in cyberspace. I was laughed at then and during the wedding speeches four years later, because when an e-mail is sent, it will be delivered and read. Now, while I listened to the teasing and laughing yet again, I felt a sense of encouragement. God had placed in me such a naïve and simple faith, even back then, which has gone on to help me over this journey and for whatever is still ahead in it. You see, I believe God is able and can intervene, and that truth helps me in many things.

It was no accident that Brett and I have the character, personalities, and life experiences we do. It's no accident that we are together and share the friendship and marriage we do. It is no accident that I have the simple faith that I do. All these things come together to enable us to walk the journey we do in the way that we do, and they help me to rely on God with utter trust and faith after almost nine years.

I'm so thankful for that and so grateful to be encouraged because I watched a DVD of a very special and fun moment in my life.

P.S. I've been thinking while prepping dinner. For those who haven't read the book and seen my struggles and doubts, I want to clarify that faith and trust have wavered, even to breaking point, but I'm thankful they are the foundation. I don't want people getting the wrong end of the stick and being hard on themselves, when I've been there myself too. Anyway, I hope that clarifies things, and I will get back to the kitchen now that I've added this.

Groundhog: August 6, 2013

I'm sure many of you on such a journey "get it"; sometimes life just feels like Groundhog Day. You have your up moments and your down moments. But every now and then you go through the same motions and wonder when they will be over.

While I am very happy in so many aspects of my life and am confident that one day we will have our miracles, this thinking doesn't alter that struggle that comes about every now and then.

You get a little tired of the following:

- Each morning getting the many bottles of vitamins, minerals, folic acid, and all that you take for laying the groundwork for that day you hope is just around the corner. They are just another reminder.

- Having yet another phone call to discuss an upcoming round of IVF and all it entails
- Facing the yearly milestone of being on this journey far too long and wondering when the finish line will be in sight
- Having yet another discussion about the future, which has so many "what ifs" and "it depends"
- Struggling through yet another weekend when you're stuck in a holding pattern. Your friends are busy doing family life, which is what you should be doing too. But instead you see all the group catch-ups you are excluded from because of your lack. Once again you are left to occupy your own time with activities you would rather not be doing.
- Getting to the point that you just can't face one more thoughtless comment, which is the blow that sends you reeling

For those who are not on such a journey, I'm sure this will just seem like a "woe is me" post, but I'm putting it out there for all who are struggling on this journey. Then you will know you're not alone, that someone else gets it. Though I mostly cope with this journey well, that's not always the case, and I wanted you to see the other side of the reality.

Who Does Know? August 19, 2013

Here I am yet again, with tears streaming down my face, as I get off the phone. Once again I've heard from the clinic that there are no answers to my "Why?"

Let me take you back a bit …

A few months back I was asked to be a leader in the children's area at a Bible study I've been going to for years. I knew my answer should be yes, but I told God I couldn't see how it would work with my pain. He told me He would take care of it. Well, I said yes and was blown away when my first period was a breeze. Then the second month, the period again was a breeze. So you can understand from experiencing such a change that I would consider the possibility of being pregnant this cycle when things unfolded as they did.

I had spotting nine days ago on a Sunday but thought it odd with my period not being due till the following Wednesday. As the week progressed, no period arrived, and the time when it should be due came and went. I became hopeful that the delay could have been from implantation and that our lives were about to change forever. Each toilet stop became filled with nerves as I wondered what I would face: hopes dashed or heightened? I decided that if it got to Monday and there was still no period, I would contact the clinic to have a blood test (as I vowed in 2010 never to go through the ordeal of a home pregnancy test again).

Yesterday being Sunday, I had more spotting and got back into bed, saying my period must be on the way, and I was devastated. I had allowed my hopes to get up once again. I had given myself permission to dwell on how we would share the news, what it would be like to have a growing belly, and what my first purchase to celebrate would be. I delighted in the fact that I would no longer feel excluded or be sent reeling by spoken words. If only I had been smarter and more cautious like Brett. I allowed myself to wallow for a few hours and then said I wanted to do something fun, only to discover that the spotting hadn't come to anything further, so hope was still on the table, and I once again found myself in a tense time.

This morning I woke and was too scared to go to the toilet but eventually needed to more than I was afraid to. I came to one more morning with no period and finally reached the moment I had set to phone the clinic. I nervously and excitedly awaited opening time only to find I needed to leave a message. I took my phone everywhere as I went about my morning tasks. At last the phone rang, and we agreed that I should do a blood test, and off I went. Then I was on with my day and waited for that all-telling phone call.

I had arranged to meet a lady through the book and was thankful she was so lovely and a welcome distraction from focusing on me. Then I went home to do my Bible study homework. Two statements really resonated and encouraged me. One was "We come to a period in Isaac's life—marked by a severe test, but also by God's personal revelation, a lapse in faith, drawn out conflicts but also of untold blessing." The other was "Do not fear for I am with you."

I looked at the clock, and my heart sank as logic told me they would have phoned the happy endings before the disappointments. I felt very deflated, as I so wanted this to be the end. Just then a lady I had supported during her IVF cycle sent me a simple text: "Psalm 20:4–5." In looking it up, I was again encouraged, especially as it was just what I needed, and she had no idea what was going on. It felt like a roller coaster ride of emotions, because moments later the phone rang, and I could hear in the nurse's voice that she didn't have good news.

I wasn't pregnant. My hormone levels showed I hadn't ovulated. That news explained why my period was elusive but didn't explain the spotting. In talking it out, I learned there was no reason for this to be such an odd cycle, and all I was told was to contact the clinic in ten days if there was still no period. They would then come up with a plan. The upcoming IVF cycle was mentioned, but that was of little comfort.

I'm okay with disappointment. I've had nine years of it. But what I hate is no concrete answers. I don't know how to work with those.

The tears are flowing. I'll feel sad for some time. I'll struggle even more with unwelcome words. I'll have a roller coaster ride of highs and lows as I try to focus on the many blessings in my life and then also think about the struggles such a journey brings. But I know without a doubt that I will hold onto hope, lean on my amazing husband and faithful God, and pull through yet again.

That Much-Needed Punch in the Face: August 26, 2013

Brett will be able to attest to me being a grumpy pants this weekend and a tad overly sensitive. Poor guy deserves a medal.

It has been a rough week. Not only did I have more disappointment and heartache with our journey, but it also came around the nine-year mark, which felt too cruel to handle.

On top of that, I felt resentful as I continued to struggle on this journey and had to listen to others moan about parenthood and experience further insensitivities.

Throw in another phone call from the clinic Friday afternoon about my upcoming IVF cycle, the continuing lack of a period, and my being offered to bring the IVF forward to start in a matter of days. This all threw me for a loop. As much as God enables me and carries me, IVF is taxing, and I need time to gear up for it, not just be thrown into it. Thankfully they accepted my request to keep it as it was, even though my mucked- up cycle will now push this into the following month.

Then those silly words from years ago taunt me while I'm down—"What have you done to deserve this?" "You just don't have enough faith; that's why it's not happening." And before you know it, I'm comparing myself to my older sister once again and feeling inadequate and inferior (she's got three amazing kids, is incredibly talented and gifted in many ways, and God is using her in a big way). And then I look at myself; other than being a good wife, sometimes I come up empty in my comparisons. She seems like the whole package who has been blessed with it all. *But what about me, God?* Maybe there is truth to those words, especially when I come up with zilch in my comparisons. Then I get on a roll and compare myself with friends too—not a great idea.

Well, thankfully today, after doing some business paper work and errands, I sat down to do my Bible study homework. As I read over the notes, the words hit me in the face like one punch after another. I realized I had once again allowed a chip to grow on my shoulder and needed to do some reconfiguring of my heart and mind, allowing God to once again smooth out the bumps I had created.

If you're in the same boat, be encouraged.

If you sometimes feel that your struggles are a punishment rather than a purpose, then check out Psalm 119:71 and John 9:3

If you think your bareness is because of a lack of faith, then read about Abraham and Sarah, and Isaac and Rebekah in Genesis, and see some incredibly godly people who struggled with just that. Then see the amazing outcome and miracle they received.

If you struggle to trust God and wait on His perfect timing, don't be tempted to manipulate it into being, as some people in the Bible did or as people in your world suggest to you. Even though it won't feel like it in the short term, in the long term you will rob yourself of God's best for you.

Each person has his or her own journey, and comparing ourselves leads only to heartache, frustration, and discontentment. You can't just look at the glossy part of someone else's life; you must look at the hardships too, just like you can't just focus on the bad parts in your life and not on the good. I don't know about you, but I'd rather stick with my life.

I am so thankful for the way God has reminded me of the many ways He has pulled through for me in the past, of the ways He has blessed me beyond measure. That reminder can give me confidence as I wait out this portion.

I am grateful that even when I let myself get pulled down, I don't need to stay there and can once again experience the joys in the now.

I'm one blessed girl.

When the Body Fails Yet Again: September 2, 2013

Over the past few months, I had the signs of things being out of whack with my skin; I looked more like a teenager than a woman. My weight went up and up no matter what, and the hair growth once again was going crazy. These changes certainly don't help one feel beautiful or feminine.

My period is still aloof, so today was another blood test to see where things are and make a plan from there. Well, the numbers are in, and once again my body fails me. I will give it another few weeks to see whether it shows up, because the hormone levels aren't conducive to manipulating it into being, as previously suggested.

I will no longer be doing the antagonist cycle of IVF as hoped, but rather I'll be starting the contraceptive pill on day four (whenever that may be) and drawing out the process of the highs of hope and the lows of fear, along with all the physical side, like more injections and the tender tummy, that comes with such a time.

Those who've done IVF get the extremes and the toll. You so desperately want to hope and believe this time could be different, to put your all into it so you know you couldn't have done any better, but at the same time there is that self-preservation of more heartache. Then there are the injections that get harder the more tender and full your tummy is, and don't forget waiting on tenterhooks for updates, which again bring highs and lows. Your body and your sense of space and dignity go out the window with all that such a time entails.

In saying all that, though, you push yourself and endure it all again and again in the hopes that this time will be different. That this time you will see your longing fulfilled, the ache replaced with joy, the struggles taken away, and the awfulness that's been endured melt away because you get to graduate.

I doubt very much I will update like I did last time, because my heart is more fragile, the struggle more acutely felt. I'll be honest; I never expected to get to nine years or to be turning thirty-four without a baby in my arms or at least on board, so it's a bigger blow than I expected. I also don't expect this to have the desired outcome, which I know sounds awful and seems like defeat. It's just that with all that's going against me, I can't see it working. This attitude is probably self-protection. I know if the pregnancy works out, it will just show how God pulled a super miracle through for me, not just a miracle. But time will tell, as that faith and hope may surge beyond reason once again, and instead of sheltering my heart, I may be brave enough to invite you along for the ride again.

What I do know is that this time I've let God know that I can't pray like I did previously; rather, I'm passing on that baton to my faithful prayer warriors, resting in the knowledge that God knows my heart. But my actions will just look a little different compared to other times. I can be assured that despite the struggles and tears, there is still that absolute conviction and belief that one day we will have our miracles. In His perfect timing and way, they will come about.

To hold onto hope in a way I can manage during this upcoming IVF cycle, I purchased some books on the anniversary of our nine years, which I plan to read aloud to my miracles in waiting. I'm doing this as a way of showing God that I'm not giving up and showing my miracles that I'm holding out to the very end. That seems more manageable than what I've invested into at other times.

This time I'm admitting my fragility. I'm relinquishing that fear that I need to do certain things or pray a certain way to see the dream realized. Rather I'm resting in the fact that none of this is in my control or on me. God is able; He will bring about the promise in His way and time. And although it's still hard, I'm okay with that, as I've finally learned that His ways really are best, even if I don't always feel this. I'm taking the pressure off me and letting go. I'm not letting go of the desire, the dream, the promise, the hope, or the faith … Rather, I'm letting go of the fear and the false notion that everything hinges on something I do or don't do. I think that in itself shows how far I've come in my relationship with God, and it reveals all I've picked up from my Bible study. At heart I'm a control freak, a perfectionist; I want to be strong and not to be beaten by anything. So for me to say, "God, here is my greatest desire. I know it's not on me to see it happen, so I give it over to You and will wait" and "I can't always be strong, and right now I'm struggling and hurting and can't see the light at the end of the tunnel" is the biggest deal ever.

Standing with You: September 18, 2013

Through this book, I've had the privilege of meeting some incredible people. I've been honored to listen over a cuppa or to read messages as they share from their hearts and let me into a very hard place. Some share about their journey of infertility; others share about losses of a loved one, the effects of serious health issues, or even struggles in friendships or parenting.

We all have different walks of life and experiences but heartache all the same. It amazes me how a book written with struggles and flaws laid bare can give opportunities for people to find they are not alone and that someone else gets it, whatever the journey. There is one lady who is heavy on my heart at the moment, as she's been dealt a blow this week with another failed IVF.

As I went about doing my housework, she kept coming to mind. Then a song came on my shuffled playlist, and I couldn't help but think how appropriate it was for her in this moment. Just then the phone rang, and it was someone going through serious health issues, and she poured out the latest bumps in her road. There are many of us who have obstacle after obstacle, and though we know they cannot be magically wiped away, it is comforting to know that someone stands with us in the hard spots. It is even more comforting to know that, though we don't get God's plan, find it unfair, and once again try to get our heads around it, our faith will anchor us if we let it.

I encourage you to listen to the song by All Sons & Daughters "Reason to Sing" and focus on the lyrics. May you be encouraged as I am each time with those words.

This post is dedicated with love to some very special people as I stand with you in this time of hardship, as I grieve with you over the latest blow, and as I pray that God will give you a reason to cling to hope once again and see the change you so desperately need.

Unable to Hide: September 27, 2013

I have found that this year hasn't been at all what I expected in so many areas. There have been some highs but also some lows. The lows have been hard, confronting, and drawn out. Even the highs have been entangled with hardships. It's not an easy place to be, and as much as I wish I could just have time out and hide from it all, I can't. All I can do is lean on each other and God, and trust that He will faithfully and graciously provide again and again.

We were scheduled for September IVF. However, my body decided to go rogue in July. My period was elusive, my hormones were imbalanced, my skin became like that of a teenage girl, my hair gain was unflattering, my weight went up by *eight kilograms* in a matter of months despite doubling my exercise, decreasing my food intake, and trying all kinds of things to get it under check.

Thursday last week I had yet another blood test to see where things were. I still didn't have the results by Friday afternoon, so I phoned the clinic to find out where things were. They had the results and had discussed a plan of action, but they had forgotten to inform the patient. I explained to the nurse that, given all that was going on with my body, we wondered whether it was wise to progress with this round of IVF and whether we were just setting ourselves up to fail. With all we have been through, that was the last thing we wanted. The agreement was that we would think about it on the weekend and let them know on Monday.

Over the weekend Brett and I discussed the round at great lengths. Finally, we decided we would indeed hold off, as my body had taken a beating, which isn't an ideal way to go into IVF. We also knew from previous advice that to gain that much weight in such a short time would adversely affect our success, and if I could lose five kilograms, we would add 2 percent to our chances. On top of that, my heart had taken a beating with more hurts and altered friendships, so to put myself through another loss at such a time was too much.

On Monday we informed the clinic that although my elusive period had arrived over the weekend and that we had been given a protocol on how to continue, we had made the call to postpone our IVF cycle. I would enroll in Sure Slim, which had come up with a program for woman with PCOS and it was based on blood results, giving us a greater chance of success with hard work and even more dedication. All that was fine until a very unpleasant phone call on Wednesday, when we received conflicting information, pressure with the current cycle, and a harsh ultimatum.

More soul-searching, tears, discussions, emotions, and prayers went into a decision yet again. I am sure many people won't understand the call we made, and that is fine, as the responsibility lies squarely on our shoulders. It is my body and our emotions that are at stake here. We don't want to wait till July 2014 (ten more months) for our next round of IVF, nor do we want to go through it when we feel we're going through the motions to see yet another disappointment, as there is too much going against us. Yes, we are past the nine-year mark now, and ten months are an incredibly long time, but big picture wise, it's better to go with our best foot forward, so to speak. We can't act out of fear and desperation; we need to act out of wisdom.

I have joined Sure Slim, and with much more discipline, blood, sweat, and tears, I trust that my hormone imbalance and weight will come into line.

Through some very timely gems at my Bible study, I have worked on the anger, resentment, and hurt that were eating away at me and causing me to be someone I didn't much care for. I know with the remainder of this study that God will continue to refine, correct, strengthen, and enable me as needed.

Some much-needed changes have and are being made to ensure that as we move forward in this time of preparation and readiness, we are in the best place we can be for ourselves and our longed-for miracles.

Grace Alone: October 15, 2013

In the past weeks I've had various contacts with women on similar journeys, whether be texts, phone calls, e-mails, or a chat over a cup of tea. It is a privilege to be able to walk beside those needing an understanding ear, and in return I found myself blessed. Some have asked me hard questions, and what I find myself answering every time is "It's by God's grace."

I'm no superwoman. I'm not someone who has unwavering strength or constant hope. I'm not someone who is able to take physical pain as if it were insignificant. I'm not someone who is able to find the good in all things. I'm not someone who is selfless and always able to celebrate everyone else's highs without feeling a pang for myself. I'm not someone who is able to give at all times. I'm certainly not someone who has it all together and is able to explain the big whys of life.

But I choose to walk with God in the ups and downs of life. I choose to seek His strength when I'm weak. I choose to pray for the hope to hang on when I'm at the end. I choose to study the Bible and find what I need. I choose to trust that in *all* things He has me, and one day I will get it.

That doesn't mean there isn't pain, tears, or struggles. It simply means that by the absolute grace of God I'm able to keep walking this journey, to find joy, to endure, to live in faith for the "one day," and to help others where I can.

This afternoon I stumbled across a clip on Facebook and thought how appropriate it was for the many who have been asking, "Where is God in all this?" I encourage you to read over the book of Job in the bible and ponder it. Just like with Job, God cannot leave us alone. I know it doesn't change the hardship, but it may help you feel like you haven't been abandoned.

Infusion of Hope: October 15, 2013

We were dealt yet another blow in the journey, and my sense of certainty in God's promise is beginning to waver. It has been over nine years with still no baby after all. What if I misunderstood? What if I wanted a baby so badly that I took things the way I wanted to and was only setting myself up for failure and heartache?

Yes, there have been amazing answers to prayer on many occasions at many crossroads (which are detailed in *A Mum in Waiting*). It seemed like there was no denying that we would indeed have children, that they would be ours in every sense of the word, and this would happen in God's time.

I couldn't help but question this momentarily at the beginning of last week. After all, I'd come across the path of many who were left with empty arms and had long moved on. Was that to be me, but I just wasn't letting go? I poured my heart out to God—my struggles, fears, needs, emotions—and said that I knew He knew better than I what we had and were going through, that He had been so faithful and had given me every reason to trust Him, but I was in need of encouragement to hold on to hope. I asked God very specifically to give me the encouragement I needed to hang on to hope, whether the promise and words were indeed true.

I asked God to do two things and for those to come from people who weren't close family or friends. First was for someone to tell me God had heard me and that there was reason to hope. Second was for someone else to give me a baby-related gift, a tangible way of holding on to hope.

Well, blow me down. That is just what I got. Honestly, after so many years of His delivering such encouragement, I don't know why it still blows me away, but it does.

I had a message from a lady whom I had briefly met, what seemed like a lifetime ago:

> I'm not sure if you remember me. I went to Papatoetoe Baptist with you guys many years ago. I have read the odd post of yours when someone shares it and been quietly following you guys. Well, I wanted to share with you that on Sunday in church during our worship, I had you very heavily come into my mind. I then started praying for you lots and had this come to me to send you a message that God hears you, He knows how you're feeling, He has you in His arms, and He wants you to hold on to Him and believe in Him that He is the giver of hope. And He has heard you, He knows your heart, your desire, and He loves

you so much. Mostly what was loudest to me and
kept repeating over and over was to tell you that He
has heard you. He has heard you. Hold onto him and
hold onto hope, because He has heard you, Natalia.

Then a lady from my Bible study, someone I hadn't had much to
do with up until last week, sent me a text. She had been on holiday
in Australia with some other ladies from the Bible study. She had
been in a store and felt impressed to buy me a wee gift. She had been
concerned that it would upset me, so she prayed about it and felt she
should make the purchase. But when she got back and showed the
other women, they said not to give it to me, as it would certainly
upset me with what was going on. She couldn't shake the feeling
that the gift was meant to be, so she was touching base to see how I
felt about it. I said I was certain it was an answer to a prayer, and my
answer was "Yes, please." The following day she passed me the gift,
saying there was no card, and she knew God would speak to me as I
unwrapped it. Well, what do you know, but it's this tiny baby doll all
wrapped up, and my heart beamed, as I knew it was "tangible hope."
It was just the infusion and confirmation I needed.

Don't think your needs are too small for God to care about.
Don't think you can't be specific with God, because it's not showing
strength or hope. As I'm learning more and more, He does care. He
is a very real, personal, and loving God who is just waiting for you
to call out.

Step at a Time: October 29, 2013

From my previous posts, you know my cycle went haywire, and
PCOS had a field day with many aspects of my body and life. As
a result, we made the hard decision and put off IVF to work on
bringing things back into line.

Thankfully Brett had heard an ad on the radio and learned
that Sure Slim dealt with people with PCOS, so off I went for my

appointment to sign up, weigh in, have blood tests done, and wait on my program to arrive to get stuck in. I felt a little silly when I got stunned reactions, as they thought I was so small to be doing a "weight-loss program," but when you've tried all you can and hormones are going nuts, you will try anything and give it your all.

The blood results happily validated that I lead a very healthy life, but the hormones were causing issues. I was also pleasantly surprised to find out how little I needed to change with my eating. The biggest thing I had to change was eating three meals a day, with five hours in between them. My protein and vegetable intake had to increase, as my portion size was apparently too small. I wasn't sure what results I could expect, but after four weeks I was very pleased to have lost 4.4 kilograms, to be sleeping better, to feel better, and for this current cycle to seem back on track.

I felt pretty excited and hopeful to reach the goal set before me

Friendships: November 6, 2013

I've had a number of messages with people this week, and there is a theme on friendships, which on such a journey can be increasingly complicated, as emotions and struggles are already heightened.

When there's been too much hurt, there's the natural tendency to doubt and question ourselves. Sadly, at times that reality also makes you wonder how to be with remaining friends, as you don't want to get that balance wrong. There is that hard balance of knowing how much to put yourself out there and wanting to pull back for self-protection.

Having a Christian upbringing and being a perfectionist at heart, I always wanted to make sure everyone was happy and would go above and beyond, often at great personal cost, as I strived to be a good friend. That made me struggle with the notion of altered friendships, as I felt like I had failed, wasn't enough, or was a bad person. I wanted to do all within my power to see the friendship survive and flourish, but in the past few years, I've realized such a desire for a friendship is not realistic or healthy. Just as others have a choice to walk away from you, you also have the choice to walk away from unhealthy and damaging friendships.

A wise and lovely elderly woman told me that everyone will let you down or hurt you at some point, because no one is perfect, ourselves included. It's how you deal with those moments that will define the friendship, for better or worse.

Let me just say that no matter your age or journey in life, everyone struggles with friendships to varying degrees, so you're not alone in this problem.

I came across the below comment, and it seemed appropriate to share with those of you who are struggling with friendships. I hope it's just the encouragement you need to know you are not the only one and to see things in a slightly different light.

> "I've decided something about friends. They all have good stuff and bad stuff. Things you like and things that annoy you. You just have to decide if you can handle their package deal."

As with most things in life, there are two sides and choices to make.

Grateful: November 19, 2013

Last night a friend of mine phoned to chat about a few things, and at the end she asked how I was. My response was "I'm *very* good. Thanks," to which she asked why. I told her the in-depth Bible study I went to was wrapping up for the year, and as I looked back over the study and the year, I could see how God's hand was on us, and I just felt good about life, despite the obvious struggles still being present.

Instead of trying to express these emotions and elaborate on what brings me to this through a blog, I wish I could sit down over a peppermint tea with you and have a good old yarn.

Anyway as I reflect on the many things that have happened over this year, I can't help but feel grateful. Amid the hardships of life are gems and blessings to be found. It's certainly not the year I had envisaged for myself, but I can certainly see that God's been with us each step of the way, going above and beyond in so many areas and graciously helping me through the tough spots.

I have been going to my Bible study for three years now, as I needed a lifeline to connect me back to God in the way I needed when I felt like I was drowning. I admit that when they said the study was going to be the book of Genesis for 2013, I thought it would be boring and wasn't so sure what I would glean from it. Well, how very wrong I was. You see God's faultless, powerful, gracious, and faithful character throughout the book. He is a God who is so personal and present, a God who provides, is purposeful, and lavishes His people with undeserved blessings. You also see a family with their many weaknesses and struggles, but God counted them as chosen, righteous, and faithful all the same. On a more personal note, you see infertility and how God gave them promises, but they took many years to come to pass. Through that you see the bigger picture and why God allowed it; through the pain there is growth and a far better future. That fills my heart with such hope and joy, because I see how that is playing out in my own journey, and it humbles me.

A lovely lady e-mailed me over the weekend, asking me how I keep going, noting that in the midst of hardship my faith is growing, and wondering what the future holds for us and whether I would ever give up. I pondered her words for a while, as I wasn't sure how to respond. For me I think it's the grace of God that has allowed me to keep going, as well as the marriage I am blessed with and the desire I have to be a mum. I think my faith is growing at this time, because from a young age, I've had a connection with God and longed for that not only to remain but to grow, so I've wrestled and pushed to see that continue when it felt like my world was falling down around me and my faith was being shaken in those hardest years. Again as I look back, I can see that God was with me the whole time, but I just didn't see His presence in the midst of my struggles.

As for what the future holds and our plans ahead, I have no idea, truth be told. There are too many "what ifs" in life, and I've come to accept that my ways are not always God's ways, so I can't get too caught up in mapping it out. We plan to continue trying for a family, taking it one step at a time and seeing how it all unfolds. And as for giving up, I can't see it happening. I believe the day is coming when I will sit with a big smile on my face, exhausted from labor but full of joy to be holding my miracles.

Another lovely lady, whom I've been walking with since the launch of the book, shared some very exciting news with me last week, and I'm over the moon for her. After a few congratulatory texts back and forth, she shared that she didn't want to share the news, as she felt it wasn't fair that she'd had success when we've been on the journey so long. My response made me realize how far my trust and faith in God have come. I told her this was right, perfect, and amazing. This was a time for her to enjoy, and there was no need to give me a thought, because whether it be when she had a cute round belly, a baby in her arms, or a toddler running around, I knew God was faithful, and His timing was perfect, and our day was coming.

Sadly, in the same week that some of the ladies I've walked with had joy, others had deep sorrow. They are heavy on my heart, and I can't help but think back over words that have been spoken in my teen years and to date—how the pain I endured wasn't about me but so I could walk with others from a place of understanding. As I've stepped out in obedience with this book and blog, I am seeing that become a reality. And while I don't have the words to take away their pain, the magic wand I wish I could wave doesn't exist. I can pray out of understanding and walk alongside them, which is what I wish I'd had in those times, so I love seeing how God works the bad for good.

This morning's devotional seems so very fitting for the grateful heart I have, despite the realities of not always being so glossy for ourselves, those we love, or those who are in our lives.

Survival 101 – Maintaining your faith while dealing with infertility: November 25, 2013

When people believe in God and life is good, life all ticks along pretty easily. It's when those hard and unexpected times in life come that throws that sense of certainty and faith. People find themselves questioning, "Is there really a God? If God is there, why don't I feel Him anymore? Why would a God who is loving and in control allow me to struggle like this?" The Bible says that He wants good for us, so how does this fit into that? The situation gets even harder when people, as well meaning as they may think they are, start adding comments that only escalate things.

I have had my fair share of moments in our nine-plus-year journey of struggling with some of those questions, frustrated at not finding the answers, feeling angry and abandoned, desperately trying to find my way forward, and holding on to the faith that is so important to my life.

When I was at my absolute lowest, I didn't know where to turn, as I didn't feel like I had found the answers I needed, but I certainly wanted to. I e-mailed our old youth pastor, John, and laid it all out on the table. Instead of what I wanted (point-by-point answers to all my questions and struggles), I got far better advice and that was to turn to the Word of God, to seek God in a very real way for myself, and I would unfold the answers I needed for myself instead of relying on others.

I admit that at first I was a bit frustrated. I'd been a Christian since I was five years old and had read the Bible many times. I'd done devotionals, attended church, prayed daily, and made God an integral part of my life. None of that had helped in my darkest hour, so where was I meant to start?

It didn't take long till I realized how incredible that advice was. It was just the kick starter I needed, and from there things unraveled to find me in a far better place with God and my faith.

Many ladies are in various parts of their journeys and struggle with similar things I did back in 2010. So there I was, giving the same advice I had been given but thought I would do a "Survival 101" in case someone is unsure what step to take to make the first move.

The Bible

I will be the first to admit that it seems daunting when you pick up the Bible, flip through it's pages, and wonder how words from long ago could be relevant to the hustle and bustle of life now. Months after I e-mailed our old youth pastor, we were in the States on holiday and caught up with them. I was able to speak to Angela, John's wife, about things more, and she suggested an in-depth Bible study that has classes in many places all over the world, and when I arrived home I signed up.

After I did three years of what I would say is an intense Bible study, the Word of God came alive in such a new way for me. Suddenly, I grew in my understanding of God, His character, my relationship with Him, and even those big questions I had about our journey. I thrived on discovering answers for myself and growing and transforming. However it works for you, I really do suggest getting into His Word for yourself and unfolding all the gems and truths, as they will astound you with how relevant they are to now. I would suggest Genesis, as there are great revelations on infertility, and also Psalms, as you see others struggle, and it's real—a great starting point, in my humble opinion.

Music

I think music is a powerful way to process the emotions and feel connection. There were days when I couldn't bring myself to pray, and all I could do was turn on my iPod and let the music and words wash over me. If you're having one of those moments, then why not at least try it? There is such great music out there, but my playlist for 'me time' consists of many songs from C3, Selah, Chris Tomlin, Jesus Culture, Hillsong, Israel Houghton & New Breed, Kari Jobe,

Planetshakers, Sidney Mohede, and All Sons & Daughters. Check them and others out and create your own playlist.

Prayer

I think prayer is hugely undervalued among so many Christians, and sadly people think it needs to be in a certain way or when you sit quietly. I pray as if I am having a normal conversation with God; it's real, and it reflects where I am. I pray when I'm cleaning, showering, and driving; and sometimes I'm on my knees. God cares so much more than we ever realize, and as you will see in previous blogs and the book, I get specific with my needs, and sometimes they are met, and sometimes they aren't. It's like a marriage or friendship. If you invest and spend time on it, then there is connection, and if you don't, then there is distance. It applies here.

Books

There are so many resources out there, and in my journey I have purchased many books to try to find what I'm looking for. I have found that these have gems hidden inside them and are just what I needed in those moments. Granted, I have purchased books, and they've sat on the shelves for years as I've needed to be in the right space, but that's okay. I just love anything by Sheila Walsh, Holly Wagner, Beth Moore, Lisa Harper, Priscilla Shirer and Joyce Meyer. Some I would highly recommend. If you want to know where to start, I would recommend the following:

> When It Pours, He Reigns: Overcoming Life's Storms
> by Holly Wagner
> The Shelter of God's Promises by Sheila Walsh
> A Woman and Her God by Beth Moore
> Stumbling into Grace by Lisa Harper
> Life Interrupted by Priscilla Shirer
> Beauty for Ashes or Never give up by Joyce Meyer

Devotional

These are important if you want to have those few moments each day, where you can glean something about God, where you can find encouragement for where you are, or a kick the butt if that's needed; then they're worth it. I love the few I've listed, as each day they give me those few moments to focus on God and my faith, and I can get what I need. It doesn't need to be some massive in-depth thing each day, just those few minutes that help you tick along. So I think devotionals are a great way to maintain your faith in the storm. Here are some titles I recommend:

> Daily Gifts of Hope: Devotions for
> Each Day of the Year by Women of Faith
> Daily Gifts of Grace: Devotions for Each Day of Your
> Year by Women of Faith
> The Women of Faith Daily Devotional
> Daily Steps for Godchicks: The 90-Day Devotional
> for Real Women by Holly Wagner

Study

As I've shared, I go to an in-depth Bible study and find that so valuable to grow me in many ways. I've also done some Beth Moore studies and know she has even more out, as do some of the other authors I mentioned. I think doing something more in depth from time to time is also a great way to keep you in the place you want to be, to help you search for what you need, and to be able to weather the storm the best you can with growing in God and all that entails. Churches and libraries actually have many of these resources, so you don't need to spend a lot when your account is likely already taking a battering with your infertility journey. It's just like a marriage or relationship. What you put in it is what you get out of it.

Mixing It Up

I find that sitting on a beach and looking at the waves crashing or being on a mountaintop and looking at the grandeur around is a great place for me to chat with God and get some perspective and understanding. Don't be limited in how you do life with God; think outside the box; keep it varied and fresh. Get on a bike and listen to a podcast of a speaker you like. Sit on a beach and listen to your favorite music. Curl up in front of a fire and read a book. Have a cup of coffee with someone you trust and can have a deep conversation with. Allow yourself to seek help from a pastor or a counselor too if you are in a place like that.

Support

I have key people in my life to whom I have sent a message to say I'm struggling and to ask them to pray because I'm just not able to. Allow others to pray for you when you can't and be there for you, as it's such a key element to it all. I pray for many people each day who've come across my path through this book and blog, and I would gladly be that person on the other end of an e-mail or text if you need specific prayer at a particular moment.

Anyway I hope this "Survival 101" is able to help some of you who I know are in that hard place I was in during 2010 and beyond. I pray that you will be able to hold onto your faith, to wade through the struggles, and to find God in a greater and more personal way than ever before, just as I have. I trust some of these tips are able to help you know what step to take. But please know that just like other relationships, there are seasons with God. There are times when you struggle, times when you feel such a closeness, times when you grow in leaps and bounds, and times when you stay put for a while.

'Tis the Season for Hope And Joy: December 8, 2013

December 1 was approaching, and excitement was building in me. I couldn't wait to put up all our Christmas decorations and to have the joy of seeing all the beautiful pieces, setting them up throughout the house, and enjoying all the season represents.

The day came, and I eagerly lay in bed, wide eyed and ready for the fun and tradition of being excited like a little kid (Brett not so much). The clock ticked very slowly past six o'clock and then seven. I didn't think it would be wise to wake him up and push him out of bed to get into it, so I waited. As I lay there, my thoughts went to the previous three years, when decorations went up late and came down early, if at all. Those were years when I was on debilitating fertility drugs and dealt some harsh blows at what can be a hard time of year when you're still left with empty arms.

I reflected on how wonderful it was not to be on fertility drugs, not to be in the process of treatment, and not to be struggling with my faith or to be in a dark space of longing and waiting. For the first time in years, that bubble of excitement was there, and I loved it.

The time finally came, and Brett was up in the ceiling, passing down the tree and boxes of decorations. It was wonderful listening to music, talking, and unwrapping each carefully packaged decoration and sprinkling the house with a season filled with hope and joy.

Now a few days later, there have been some developments, and I find myself sitting here with my heat packs and curled up on the couch, writing. But I look at my beautiful tree (in particular the angel) and my heart beams with joy and hope. I can't help but think how that angel with the trumpet of praise and thanksgiving represents how I feel so well.

As you know, I deal with endometriosis and PCOS. My body certainly likes to do its own thing, and there doesn't seem to be any understanding it. In September, when we were meant to do our third round of IVF, my body went rogue for a few months, and we delayed IVF till the following year while we focused on losing the weight hormones created and getting my cycle in line. I am pleased to say that at the moment I have lost ten kilograms and am well on track for IVF. I was excited when the last cycle, after a three-month stretch, went straight back into line and wrongly assumed that would continue. However, this cycle was forty-four days!

Due to the earlier incident, I didn't go down the road of "what if," and my body certainly didn't give me anything that got me hopeful or expectant that this could be our time. On Monday, when we were at the forty-three-day mark, I sat there, having done my devotional. The words were "And the scripture says that Jesus was life and the light of all of us, which means that everything that has breath has originated from him." I get specific with God, and sometimes He answers the way I want, and other times not so much. I told Him that with His power and forming of life, I would like my period to arrive by the end of the day; and if I was to wake the following one without it, then I wanted the delay to be because this was our time, not because this was dragging out.

Well, the following day I woke, and there was still no period, but I had a sense it wasn't going to pan out the way I had prayed, and there was an acceptance. I wasn't frustrated or disappointed. God has taught me through the ups and downs of this year that even when things don't make sense, even when things don't go our way, He is still in control. His ways are still far better than ours, and there is every reason to keep trusting Him and walking with Him. So that is what I was going to do.

Later, I was in Albany, doing my groceries after my Sure Slim appointment and getting the last gift needed, when the pain in my back and tummy started. I knew that when I got home, it would be all go with my period, and sure enough it was. I know many may be frustrated on my behalf or feel bad for me, but there is no need for that. This morning the verse in my devotional was "To You they cried out and were delivered: In You they trusted and were not disappointed" (Ps. 22:5).[3]

How very fitting those words of encouragement are to me at this moment. As I continue trusting in God for the promises He has given, I will *not* be disappointed. 'Tis the season for hope and joy in every respect. I look back over this year and am amazed at what God has done and am so humbled and overwhelmed. It makes me so full of joy, so hopeful and expectant for whatever my New Year holds.

Life may have dealt you some blows this year; you may be approaching the time when family is key with empty arms too. But can you see beyond that and know that Psalm 22:5 is relevant for you too? I hope so, I truly do. My thoughts are with so many of you, especially at this time of year.

"I Love Love": December 20, 2013

Last night Brett and I went out to dinner and then attended an Alicia Keys concert. As we headed off into the city, we reflected on the year and talked about a family who has an "end-of-year work dinner," a tradition when family members reflect on the year that has been and set goals for the new year. They spend time as a family and intentionally build on that. I mentioned how awesome many of their family traditions are and that I couldn't wait to do some of theirs and our own. As it turned out, given the way our dinner conversation went, we in affect had our own family work dinner.

In February we will be married eleven years, and while this year has had its struggles and we are still left with empty arms in one sense, it is by far my favorite year. I have seen my relationship with God increase, I have seen myself grow as a person in many ways, and I've seen my amazing marriage go to an even greater level through that. There have been many, many highs amid some of the lows. And I can't help but be full of thanksgiving for this year and have such hope and expectation for the next, regardless of what it holds. I know things will only get better.

While I'm sharing, let me give you a small glimpse into the way I've grown in God and in myself, and how that has filtered into my marriage by sharing this wee story. I am a very strong-willed person at times, and sometimes that isn't a good thing. Some months back I had a tumor in my ear canal removed by surgery and admit I was very blasé about it. I insisted that with all Brett had going on, he didn't need to come, and I also was in task mode and wanted to get certain errands done beforehand. However, this didn't stop me from being disappointed when Brett headed out the door for his frantic workday and forgot to wish me good luck.

As I went about my tasks, I spent a few minutes feeling annoyed about this, especially after being so accustomed to his lavishing love and care. But then I realized he would likely phone me while I was headed in, which would be nicer. When the time came for me to head in and I still hadn't heard from him, I decided that I had a choice to make. I could be stubborn and take offense, having a sulk about it and letting him bear the brunt of it when he came home. Or I could phone him, tell him I needed him to wish me luck, and hear him tell me it would be okay. I decided that, with the marriage we had, knowing the character of my husband and thinking on how God had been growing me and what I'd learned about offenses in my Bible study, instead of having a sulk, I would pick up the phone. So that is just what I did, and I love how the call took our marriage to that next level and how it has altered those little grumbles that can happen when two people do life together.

Anyway, back to the evening … The concert was amazing! Alicia Keys's incredible voice belted out soulful songs about love and life. At times the words caused my heart to bubble over with joy as I sat next to the man of my dreams, holding his hand and loving what we shared, how far we've come, and all that lay ahead. There was a couple two rows down who were so into the concert and clearly very happy in what they shared, and I love that; it's not often that you see people who are head over heels. Then Alicia's backup singers turned out to be married to each other, and he said, "Help me sing this song to my wife." I leaned over and said, "I love love" because I do; I truly love love … in all forms of the word. I love how God loves us. I love how Brett and I love each other. I love how I know I will love my miracles so overwhelmingly. I love that there are so many levels of love and that it makes the world a better place. I just love love; I always have, and I always will.

The best part of the night would have to be when Alicia's child came on stage, and my eyes welled up with happy tears. I loved that this family toured together and allowed their child to be part of this world. I love how my very being leaped with hope and expectation for the day our worlds would change with the arrival of *our* miracles, whenever that day may be.

At the end of the concert, Alicia said, "Celebrate love. Celebrate life, and you can be sure it will only get better" as she sang her final songs.

I couldn't help but think about those words "Celebrate love and celebrate life." How very fitting it is that this Christmas I am excited, and for the first time in years I'm looking forward to Christmas. Even more so, we purchased a wee gift to go in our stockings, and it holds such significance. To you they may seem like a wee Mickey and Minnie. But to me they signify thanksgiving for this amazing year and God's faithfulness through the ups and downs. They signify the hope and expectation that are very much alive at this time of year, instead of great sadness that on such a family-orientated day, when we celebrate the birth of our Savior, we are still waiting. No, this year we mark the closing of one year and the beginning of another as we do celebrate love and life, as we are full of thanksgiving and hope.

The best is yet to come. I know it.

The Dawn of a New Year: January 1, 2014

At the stroke of midnight dawned a new year. The "celebration" would have looked different for many. Some of you may have been surrounded by family and friends to see in a new year. Others may have been like us and headed to bed earlier, having spent the evening as just the two of you.

It's a time of year when you reflect on what has been and look ahead to a fresh new year, one full of possibilities. I know all too well that each New Year has its highs and lows. I know that some of you have your long-awaited miracle and are on a mountaintop, heading into the year, which I couldn't be happier about. I know others of you are in a place where appointments, treatments, and procedures loom and bring many emotions as you embark on this next step in the journey, and I feel for you and hope you know I'm here.

While I look back over my year and feel truly grateful and blessed for what God has done, there is still that longing for my babies, wondering whether this dawn of a new year will finally see the dream realized. The old saying "Pictures paint a thousand words" has made me share what's below instead of putting my highlights into words.

Hope gifted to us during IVF

The land we found on the day IVF failed, a haven to call home

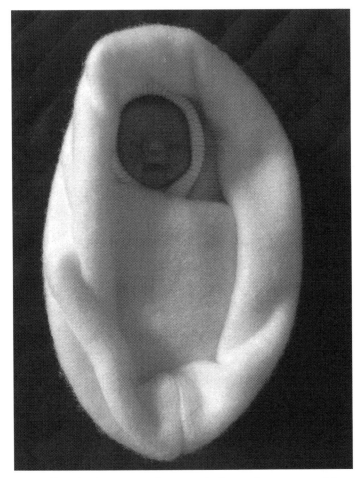

The doll gifted to me when I cried out for renewed hope

Brett gets a bike to inject fun back into our world.

Us once again living, about to head to a concert

My hope for all of you is that this year will be one filled with blessings. May you find a greater depth and growth in God, and experience joy and love while walking with those special people by your sides as well as adventures to be experienced, dreams realized, and more highs than lows. Here's wishing you a bright 2014. May it be your greatest year yet in all areas of life, however that looks for each of you.

Tug-of-War: January 28, 2014

Words and actions of others shape you for better or worse. For as long as I can remember, this reality has created an internal tug-of-war in my life.

"If you won't do it perfectly on your first try, then don't try." is the saying that seems passed down the generations on my mum's side and one I heard her say often without realizing.

The countless comments made by family, friends and strangers over the years that were belittling my singing to God, praying to God, sharing God with others, or mentioning how much my faith is the core of my life only led to my getting quieter and quitter, almost to being silenced until God did a work to alter that back to what He had created in me.

Watching on as people close to me were in ministry and seeing the elements of burn out, being lonely, put on a pedestal, or being so consumed by their calling that the family is abandoned and hurt. I even experienced a small taste myself when I did a short internship at the church in my youth, where I vowed at the end never to be a leader or serve in any capacity.

All the above created in me a desire to walk with God but not be part of any ministry, so much so that when Brett and I were talking marriage, I triple-checked that there was no deep-down desire or calling on his life that would hinder that plan of a simple and ordinary existence I'd set out.

Some may see my words as comical given the words given over the years about our family having an impact on others and God using our struggles to help others. But in my mind that simply means that in the comfort of our home, we could welcome people, listen, and walk beside them. The way we were in our marriage and the way we want to be as a family could be an encouragement to them.

While there have been other words given to me that quite honestly scare me, I simply labeled those as misinformed and stuffed them way down into a dark corner, never to be reheard, resurface, or become a reality.

Yes, you can laugh that my plan and my simple life haven't panned out as I ordained. Rather, I can see how God has orchestrated His plan instead. It took me two years of being defiant, struggling, and second-guessing till *A Mum in Waiting* was written, and then there was again some feet dragging to get it out there. But even then, I said, "Okay, God, I will do this book, but then that's it. My work is done." But it seems not, as a blog continued it, and then even that didn't see it stop.

Last year God stirred me and worked on me. Since being in the in-depth Bible study, I had a number of people telling me I was made for leadership and that I should really serve as one at the bible study. Each time I said, "No thanks" and then eventually said, "Just because I'm able doesn't mean I should, and until God tells me Himself, then the answer is a big no."

In April last year I ordered a bunch of books from Amazon. I'd already read them years before but had given them away. I had since decided that I should create a library of these books to lend out to women I come across through the book and blog. As I was ordering them, I decided that being in a different space of life, I would look to get some books for me.

T. D. Jakes's book *God's Leading Lady* popped up in my search. My heart started racing, and I reluctantly read the blurb. I knew from my racing heart that God wanted me to read this book, so I purchased it (but it sat on the bookshelf till this month). While I realized God was at work, I again dragged my feet in defiance, though that didn't stop Him from progressing.

As you know, in July last year I was asked to serve as a children's leader. Tears streamed down my face, and I told God, "No way!" However, given the way the opportunity all came about and what God was speaking to me, I knew my answer should be yes. So I went into the role and turned out loving it and being so greatly blessed by it. Still in my stubborn way, I told God, "It's okay to do this, but after that no more, okay? I draw the line here. Honestly, don't expect any future obedience, however slow or quick, 'cause I'm out." I can just picture God laughing at me, for He knew better.

The year progressed even more, and by the end of the year, I shared at the in-depth Bible study I go to. I said that 2013 hadn't been the year I had laid out for myself, but God had far better plans for me. I grew in God and myself even more, and now I trusted Him to lead me on a whole new level. Finally, after being a Christian for twenty-nine years, I felt His unconditional love, saw how deeply faithful He was, knew that even in the pain His plans are better, realized the weight of His blessings and provisions, and understood that I could trust Him wholeheartedly in whatever was ahead.

These events led me to pick up *God's Leading Lady* and start reading it over the holidays. I was so excited as I turned the pages that I posted this on the *Mum in Waiting* Facebook page: "I am currently reading *God's Leading Lady* by T. D. Jakes and am loving it. When I'm done, I'll write a blog to take you behind the scenes, so to speak. But I just had to share this from page 109: "Are you willing to be misunderstood by others who can't fathom the cost of what you've been given by your God? Are you willing to risk their condemnation and attempts to silence and shame you back into your past on the other side of town?"[4] WOW! I finally am. How about you?

And while I'm not yet finished with the book, I thought I would take you behind the scenes to show you what God can do. He can take a girl who flat out refused, to be in the place of "Here I am."

I have no idea what God has in store for me or for us as a couple or family. I'd be lying if I didn't admit that the possibilities scare me a bit. But I know God is gentle with me and takes me in baby steps, because that is how I'm wired.

I love that God can use my flawed and ordinary self for others.

Rays of Hope in the Waiting: February 10, 2014

Recently, Brett and I had a three-day weekend up north in and around Paihia to celebrate our eleventh-year wedding anniversary. I feel so blessed to walk this life with my extraordinary husband and love celebrating these milestones. It was such an amazing weekend.

However, short, sharp waves seemed to interrupt the fun and celebrations at times, as if I were on a warm beach and freezing water were lapping over my feet. I couldn't help but feel the harsh reality sweep over me. The start of a new year, the milestone of another anniversary, is all wonderful and full of goodness. But underlying it is also this nasty reminder that here we are yet again with empty arms and unknowns ahead. The year 2014 is the ten-year mark of trying for a family, which I certainly hope we don't reach but know all too well could be a reality. The situation is all so unfathomable to me. We are in territory most people don't come near; the gap between our existence and that of those around us is widening. I can't allow myself to get sucked into all the emotions and fears; I just can't go there, so I try to grasp at hope and truth and strength, clinging to my God and willing His grace to sustain me yet again.

The week that followed was one in which there were rays of hope streaming through reality, each lifting my spirits that much more.

The first ray of hope started with the lyrical notes of children playing and laughing wafting through the air. Our home is near a school and kindergarten, and until the beautiful sounds once again filled the air, I didn't realize how much I'd missed them with the holidays. How good for my soul this was.

Then I touched base with a lovely lady who had an adorable "baby bump" and shared some photos; she had gone from fear to the enjoyment stage after a long road to getting her miracle. My heart beamed, and I felt so thankful for being able to join in the joy stage of those I've walked the pain stage with through this page and book.

The following day I was reading material and came across this perfectly appointed message as I was flitting back and forth from resignation to hope, frustration to peace:

> You are free to know, love trust and obey God. As you trust God's love for you, you respond with love for Him, which pours forth to others. Expressions of thankfulness in all circumstances reflect the deep joy of the Holy Spirit. You can be confident that God

has not forsaken you. You can experience genuine security. You can also experience the joy of knowing that suffering is neither meaningless nor endless; it will bring blessing to others and to you, and eternal glory to God. God will not allow suffering to continue one minute longer than necessary to fulfill His perfect purpose for you. The joy of conscious fellowship with Jesus produces a recognizable peace and absence of worry when faced with the challenges and difficulties of life. You can trust that God will not mock or betray you but will carry you through to triumph.

Later I was sitting at a lunch with a bunch of ladies I love, and a cute, little toddler in Minnie clothes caught my eye out the window. As my mind flitted to "one day," she turned around, and I realized it was the little girl of some dear friends. It couldn't have been a more perfect week to have a "chance" meeting, see their smiling and understanding faces, have a cuddle with a spunky and adorable toddler, and once again lift my spirits yet another notch.

The next day I was out doing errands on Waitangi Day (a public holiday in New Zealand), when a sharp pain consumed me. I usually had a warning, and the pain would build up, but this time while driving home from the PO box, I found myself clutching the steering wheel, crumpled in an awkward position, as a terrible period once again halted my plans. Brett was working, as we'd planned a fun day for Friday to make it another fun, long weekend. I knew he wouldn't be home for hours and that my plans were now turned upside down, as I would be relegated to the bed with painkillers and heat packs. I decided to muster up the strength, dragged myself into the DVD store, and rented the cheesy Christmas movies I'd been too busy to watch at the right time of year. This would at least bring me some joy as I bore the all-too-familiar agony of the month. Once home I got the DVD in, took the painkillers, heated the heat packs, and crumpled into a heap on my bed.

But the DVD wouldn't play, and the tears flowed. I'd mustered all the strength I could to do what I had, and I was out. I needed my babe home. While he couldn't change my circumstance, having him by my side was always the best medicine. When he knew I was suffering like this, he always came home early, but I knew his workload and decided to just put a feeler out instead, thrilled to find he would be home soon. I crawled along the floor from the bedroom to the lounge, with the DVD and heat packs in hand. Collapsing into the beanbag with the movie finally working. As I watched, my heart once again beamed. This family in the movie experienced a Christmas miracle, and it brightened my spirits to know the impossible can happen. While I clutched my stomach, my spirits lifted; while this pain may be my reality now, it wasn't always to be. There was reason to hang on to hope for our miracles, to know God would keep His promises, even if they weren't in the time and way I wanted.

Well, as the movie progressed, my phone went off. I received a beautiful photo of an adorable, little baby girl. A lady I'd met through the book had her precious miracle and was sharing the news with me. I was delighted. After a few texts back and forth, I would have the joy of meeting up with them for a catch-up after she'd settled into her new life; I couldn't wait. As I stared at the screen for probably the tenth time, my heart swelled with hope, longing, and anticipation; and I felt so blessed that this message had come through at the perfect time.

More days passed, and I was at my adored niece's eighth birthday party. The girlie fun, the games, the chatter, the giggles, and even the opportunity to join in on it all, as one of the girls wanted a buddy for the games, was an absolute delight. The simple pleasures of the day did my heart good. I loved watching my sister do the mum stuff and admired the way she and her husband are parenting these three amazing kids. I got to go to the supermarket with the birthday girl and my babe to pick the ice cream for dessert. All this made my heart sing for "one day" and reminded me why we endure all that we do for what is coming. The small and simple things that come with kids will make this worth it.

A few more days passed, and I got a text from my dear friend, saying she'd heard a verse in church and wanted to share it with me, as we came to mind when she heard it. Habakkuk 2:3 says, "For the revelation awaits an appointed time; it speaks of the end and will not prove false. Though it linger, wait for it; it will certainly come and will not delay."

So in one week I had many rays of hope in the midst of waiting. "Thankful" is an understatement. While I don't know how this year will unfold, I hang onto hope. While it feels like we are at a stalemate as we await action, I will cling to the good and known. While I keep taking it a step at a time and walking a journey I never wanted, I think and pray for many of you each day, trusting that you too will find your happy ending sooner than later. I'm praying that you and I will have many rays of hope as we continue to wait.

Realigning: March 3, 2014

No matter how strong our walk with God is or how secure we feel in ourselves and our lives, there are those times when the darkness overshadows the light and we need to realign ourselves and allow God's truths to once again take place.

Just last weekend, I spent much time responding to a lovely lady who wrote about her struggles. I shared that God is faithful even when we are not. I told her she was loved, cherished, and chosen; I shared many other amazing truths in response to her questioning and struggles. I shared with her that Satan loves to wheedle his way in with lies and taunts and that we need to replace them with God's truths. The irony isn't lost on me; days later a flu knocked me out. I was laid up in bed and struggling to focus on the truths instead of the taunts while I was weary.

While I was feeling frustrated about the promises for our miracles but the reality of being in what feels like a very long and hard holding pattern, I spoke to God. Why did things have to turn with someone praying for healing last year for my painful periods, with His telling me that with taking on kids' leadership at my Bible study that I didn't need to worry about the debilitating pain, with months of enjoying the freedom of normal periods and basking in the wonder of it all? During periods I got shaky and kept thinking about the book from John Bevere on intimidation, so I prayed. But with each month, my situation got worse and worse to the point that once again I was bedridden and in unbearable pain.

I admit that I just threw in the towel at that point. "Okay, God. If this is my lot, then fine. It's too long of fighting too many battles to be bothered." Well, this week, finding time on my hands and mulling over many things, I brought this issue to God's attention. I knew another period was looming, and with the Bible study being back on after months of holidays, the situation just wasn't workable. God didn't tell me off. He just softly said, "My child, the healing is yours for the taking, but you let fear rob you of it. You think if you are healed but _____ and _____ don't come that Satan and other people's words will hold truth. You think your heart can't take that blow and that it's better to deal with the pain you do know and handle. I have promised you the miracles, and in My timing, it *will* happen, so step out, enjoy the healing, and find the joy in growing in me while you wait and trust that I have this, and I mean *all* of this!" Mmmm. That message sent me reeling and gave me many things to mull over. It wasn't really the response I'd expected.

I started out this year with many hopes and dreams. I wanted to see change and growth. I wanted to see things really progress on so many fronts. Yet as the weeks went by, I didn't see things unfold as I had hoped. Yes, yes, I know. It was only the beginning of March and only two months after the New Year, but patience has never been one of my virtues. While I was laid up in bed, I realized that walls I'd put up due to hurt would hinder some of those things, that fear of the unknown wasn't going to get me there either. So this morning, while my body is physically on the mend, I'm seeking to realign my heart, soul, and spirit to be on the mend too so that this year can truly be all I want and more.

Are there things you know you need to realign too? Are some things so deep down but you're too hesitant to even go there? Well, my friend, let's be brave together, take the plunge, and see how things unfold from here. I am sure they will be beyond our wildest dreams. I'm certain the situation won't all be as we've wanted, but I'm pretty confident it will be even better in the long run.

Misplaced Blame Game: March 10, 2014

In our long journey, those who believe in God and those who don't have asked me the loaded question in many forms. "What have you done to deserve this?" It's as if people think that infertility is punishment for some wrongdoing. If you've been asked this question enough times, you begin to wonder if there is truth to it.

I came to peace with this element when I studied the Word of God and got to know His true character and heart. Things I'd picked up from others' misguided words and my misconstrued notions over the years became clear. But the searching I had in my heart, the despair, and condemnation I've felt have been what I've seen in those who have been struggling and touching base with me of late.

Imagine my absolute delight when I read the Bible just now and came across this:

"In the time of Herod king of Judea there was a priest named Zechariah, who belonged to the priestly division of Abijah; his wife Elizabeth was also a descendant of Aaron. *Both of them were upright in the sight of God, observing all the Lord's commandments and regulations blamelessly. But they had no children, because Elizabeth was barren;* and they were both well along in years" (Luke 1:5–7, emphasis added).

Here are two people who were blameless before God, and even they experienced infertility. It wasn't punishment. It wasn't deserved. They had done no wrong to cause this. The simple fact was, it was an element of their lives. I don't know about you, but that excited me because it seemed like vindication for me and all those who've reached out for answers in their struggle.

While I can't return the words that have been spoken to me or you, what I can do is give some of you that much-needed validation through sharing this verse. I hope this helps you shake off those misplaced words and realize you don't need to carry the weight of that guilt anymore.

It breaks my heart how much people's misplaced words affect others or how much someone carries guilt and struggles needlessly. This problem doesn't just apply to infertility, by the way; I know from experience that it can relate to more than that. So I trust that you will find peace and validation through this and can put aside that burden that was never yours to carry.

What Are You Hearing? April 2, 2014

Last night after dinner, Brett said he needed to pop to a building site to check that all was good for the team to stand frames the following day. I enjoy any activity with my man, so I happily went to check it out with him. We then carried on to another job to check on something else and were having a great time chatting about all kinds of things, with much laughter along the way. I had joked about his owing me an ice cream cone, so we stopped in to get gas and some treats on our way home. I guess I was beaming from the fun with my babe, because the guy at the counter started up the usual polite conversation one has. "How is your day going?"

"Really good, thanks. How about you?"

And this was when everything changed. His response was "So-so until you came in."

And I heard depression from his thick accent and said, "Oh, that's not good," and then he clarified what I'd thought I heard and what he'd actually said. "I was refreshed." Well, that seemed better. I got back into the car, and Brett commented on the laughter happening between the guy on the counter, myself, and the guy behind me, so I filled him in.

The situation got me wondering about what we perceive and what is reality. It can be a word not understood, a comment overheard and taken out of context, a misinterpreted look, or someone's hurtful words that are taken to heart when in reality he or she is lashing out because of his or her issues, which have nothing to do with you. Words are spoken, gestures or expressions are given, and sometimes there is intended sting behind them, but other times we are the ones who get the communication muddled up. The intended and unintended shape the way we view ourselves and even others. The good and bad leave an impression on our hearts.

This issue even goes a step further when God wants you to hear His truths and Satan wants to counteract them with lies. Depending on what you focus on, this can hugely impact your self-esteem, the way you live out your life, how you react to others, and so much more.

So what are you hearing?

One of *Those* Moments: April 14, 2014

I have loved life even more so than usual these past months. Yes, there are always little glitches that happen, but on the whole it's been awesome to enjoy getaways with my man, to see progress on the house front, to set goals on the business side, and just to have fun and also see the potential in all that lies ahead.

I've felt so full of hope for this year and next, imagining us building and moving into our new home; having a big, round belly; and becoming a family of four and so much more. I know, time is flying, and before you know it, August will be here, and we'll see the ten-year mark on this journey of trying to conceive. Then just after that, I become thirty-five years old, which is so different compared to how I pictured being at that stage. I know it seems naïve to think my happy ending is just around the corner, as I've imagined scenarios and been full of hope countless times, only for it to once again not come to pass. I have no idea what God's timing and plan are. But that fact doesn't stop there being such a sense of anticipation for this year and the next, whether it unfolds as I picture it or not.

Just the other week I had three people ask me where things were at with our journey and upcoming treatments, and I said that the July IVF was still a go, but for now I was loving life and felt like I was on holiday, despite life's busyness. My body didn't have to endure treatments, my emotions didn't need to deal with the punches, and it just felt nice. They all commented on how that fact shone through, that I was just me and enjoying life and all it held.

Given all that, I didn't expect the weekend we just had. But for those who may not be in the know, I'll explain a little bit first. During our first round of IVF in 2011, two embryos didn't make it to implantation. Viewing them as life and not wanting the clinic to simply discard them in the waste, we brought them home, took a moment, and buried them in the red rose pot plant. In 2013 six more embryos were added to the pot. Each day I water the roses, and most of the time, we don't give the matter any thought.

After several years it seemed the rose bushes didn't like being in the pot plants and were no longer thriving. Still I continued to care for them, but last week Brett told me they were dead, and it was time to replant more. This news made me reflect on what was buried beneath the soil and how we would need to source them and bury them with new soil and plants. The situation also made me think about how much this journey affects us, about how many things "die" as a result of it—dreams, hopes, plans, even friendships, and so much more. Yes, we grow stronger, we find the good in the bad, and we find new dreams, adjust our hopes and plans, and keep on going for "one day." Mingled in the heartbreak is growth, and amid the loses are gains, but for better or worse, we are forever changed.

Anyway, I digress. As I was saying, with how well life was going, I didn't expect the tears and heartache that came this weekend from doing the gardening. We got on our work clothes and discussed the plan of action, and without knowing why, my stomach began churning; the tears were flowing before I even stepped outside. I couldn't articulate why as I wiped them away and tried to get words out to my concerned husband. I thought I had grieved those losses in 2011 and 2013; I had thought that pain was no more, but it hit me once again.

Not long after that, I stood there in the backyard with the two tubes (picture if you will a small cylinder that is about the size of a pencil, clear plastic, and inside wrapped in tissue are these tiny little embryos that are now blackened dots) in hand and the nurses' notes on them. I remembered the days I'd been passed them, the days we'd buried them, for they were part of us and couldn't be discarded or forgotten. How brutal this road can be at times. My current period ensured another "dream" was lost. My hands held tubes that represented such heartache and loss. I remembered words my friends had spoken during those losses, of my having my first born with their second or third child, as they tried in vain to make those blows bearable. How far that is from how events have all unfolded isn't lost on me either, with us still with empty arms and them with numerous children, most at school age. Oh, how many hopes and dreams felt lost as I stood there, reeling in all the memories, emotions, and the great pain of it all.

This weekend I've had one of *those* moments that bring reality back into play. But as I wipe even more tears as I sit here and type, I hold onto new hopes, dreams, realities, and possibilities. While I feel the blow of this reminder, I know with certainty that God is faithful, that He *is* in control, that His timing *is* perfect, that He *does* carry us in the realities and pain of this journey, and that "one day" *is* coming. While there will always be an imprint of this experience on our hearts, it will have brought about a family that can attest to the goodness of God, the beauty in life, and the blessings that are birthed out of hardship.

This post is dedicated in honor of the precious lives and the hopes and dreams lost by all those who have walked, or are walking, on such a journey.

Others may not know the pain or gravity; those around you may seem to have forgotten; but today it is honored and remembered.

Tearing Down Walls: April 30, 2014

I don't know about you, but when I experience deep hurts, I build a wall. It wasn't until my Metformin year that I realized the reality of why and the consequence of doing so.

I can remember as a child sitting on the bed in tears. My parents wanted to know what was going on, and I placed a wall of pillows around myself, because the innocence of my childhood had been stolen from me. There was trauma I couldn't comprehend, and my way of coping was to push people away, build a wall of protection, and create independence. This behavior wasn't healthy, but as a small child, it was my coping mechanism.

This habit carried on into my teen years and adulthood. People deeply hurt me in many facets, and that sense of independence grew stronger; those invisible walls were built taller.

When I married, I was blessed with a man who was very aware, and he said, "I'm not going to let you build a wall and keep me out. It's not going to work with me." His determination, his wisdom, and the depth of his love ensured he was the only person who wasn't walled out.

Over the years, God has been doing a great work in me. As He felt I could cope, He brought to mind a memory I had stuffed down, forcing me to deal with it head on, to process it and find another level of healing and freedom. He has allowed me aha moments when I've comprehended my actions and reactions, what they stem from and how to change them. Through that experience, He has been taking one brick down at a time and allowing me to see my need for connection, my need to trust, and my need to deal with these. Then I can show my miracles the better way of living life and not robbing themselves of the fullness of life God has for all of us if we would just let down those walls.

I knew there was a biggie left to confront and that I couldn't do so on my own. My sister suggested going to someone for ministry, and with much hesitation, I finally took the leap this month. The funny thing is, as I headed there, I had this fear that the person would say I was too messed up and ask me to go away. I thought back to the time before God had begun His great work and not to the truths of now. I went in, sharing very little and wanting to ensure that their words were from God speaking to them and that the prayer for ministry was God's leading. The irony is that even in that situation, there was a bit of a wall. But God did a beautiful thing as the anger and feeling abandoned, unprotected and unloved by my parents for the abuse they didn't notice or protect me from began to dissolve. The unhealthy patterns they had allowed for our upbringing and the hole that left began to heal. Leaving space for a better relationship with my parents to begin. They spoke words I knew were from God, and best of all, I felt God's gentle whisper saying, "You don't need walls anymore."

Each person has been through hurts to varying degrees; this is part of life. Some people's blows aren't as significant as others, but they all leave an imprint, sometimes a scar. I've come to realize that I'm not the only one who has put up a wall of protection or unhealthy coping mechanisms in place; and while I get it, the time will come when God will gently work on you and say it's time to tear down the walls, to find healing, freedom, and a better life.

If you are one of those people, no matter which part of the continuum you are on, be encouraged that you're not alone, that there is hope. And when we let God work, beautiful things happen.

Philippians 1:6 says, "For I am confident of this very thing, that He who began a great work in you will perfect it until the day of Jesus Christ."

Worthy of More: May 13, 2014

Let me paint you a picture as I take you back to my childhood and show you how I was made up in an attempt to show you that people often mistake a socially strong person for someone having great confidence and self-esteem. But I also desire to convey just what God has done.

While I don't remember, I've heard stories of when I was a toddler and didn't want to miss out on the fun. When I was put to bed, I kept coming out to be able to be part of all the fun with the guests. I'd make up the need for a drink and have a sore elbow or knee. Finally, I'd be put back to bed yet again and fall asleep. I've heard how I captured the room and stole the spotlight with my antics.

Jump forward many years. At the age of thirteen, we returned to New Zealand. On my first day of school, some girls asked me to join their group at lunchtime. I gratefully accepted, only to find that all they did was sit there in the "popular zone" and pick at people's appearances. On the second day of school, I chose to roam and find other friends. In class afterward, they asked what had happened, and I simply said I didn't want to spend my lunchtime pulling people apart or having friendships like that. From the astounded response, I gathered it wasn't normal to deny being chosen by this group.

Despite my bubbly personality, in which I made friends easily, my firm foundation of right and wrong and my God-given ability to stand by my convictions no matter what flack I got didn't change what lay beneath. The abuse I experienced and the things I saw tainted my perceptions; they all worked together to create a girl who loathed herself, harbored great insecurity, and believed many lies.

By the time we moved to Auckland for my final year of school and I met Brett, there lay behind the exterior of a happy, outgoing girl a very fragmented one. I remember when we started going out that he had his work cut out for him. First, he worked on pulling my hand away every time I smiled or laughed so my mouth could be seen. Bit by bit, between God working and Brett helping to alter my self-view, lies were replaced with truths. I discovered that I was worth something; I did deserve to be loved. As I shared in a previous post, Brett was the only one not walled out, and I relished his love, adoration, and the way he treated me like a princess; he made me feel so secure. I thrived in that attention, and my self-esteem and confidence grew. Those, in turn, overflowed to other areas of life, and I felt like I'd found my groove.

Sadly, because of some lies that were so deeply engrained and continued hurts from others, I still had some hang-ups. In 2010, when Metformin days hit and I saw everyone in my infertility support group get her miracle, I began to believe another lie. It wasn't until the catch-up to meet babies and a conversation with one of them that I realized it, though. I felt so blessed to have the relationship I did with Brett and thought that maybe because what we shared was rare, it was the only blessing allotted to me, and it was for others to have the enjoyment of babies. I know, you may wonder how I could possibly think that when God has continually given words about our family not only being but also being used to impact others, being given back tenfold for what has been endured and so forth. But there you have it; lies don't make sense, and they don't fit in with known truths.

In 2011 I joined a Bible study, which helped me sift through more lies for truths, learn the real character of God, and be able to walk with Him in a new, real, vibrant, and deep way. Through the study of Isaiah in 2011 and Acts in 2012, I saw God in a new light. In 2013, with the study of Genesis, I began to see our journey and God's unconditional love for me in a new way too. It was so freeing to be able to be in this better place, and I thought my sense of worth had been fine-tuned in its entirety.

I shared in a previous post about having prayer and sensing that the walls were no longer needed. But I also had another massive breakthrough I've been mulling over, and now I feel the need to share it. Now you have the backstory; here goes.

I was asked during that time of ministry mentioned earlier, what lie I was believing, and out of my mouth popped, "I'm not worthy of more blessings"; and as the couple and I prayed and talked through various issues, I was able to come to a place where every fiber of my being knew that God said, "You are worthy of more," and the tears flowed. I already feel so greatly blessed and am humbled to think that God loves me so much, that with all He's already given, there is yet more.

Call me crazy, but as I mulled over this truth, I began to feel guilty and had to work through it to accept more. Yes, I know I'm still on this heartbreaking journey of infertility, and I know that with the many blows life has dealt me and us, it doesn't make sense. My heart has always been about people, though, and so it grieved me that others have also endured problems, and I want them to get the same reassurances, promises, and blessings. I like things to be fair, despite knowing life is far from that. I needed to work through that issue before I could share this, though; thanks to my wise man and gracious God, I did on Friday evening, so I decided it was time to share.

Every single person has been through hardships and as a result has things to deal with. That is sadly part of life in this world. Some people choose to seek God and walk with Him as a result, and others don't. But today I want to share with you that God loves you, even if you don't reciprocate. He has chosen you, and He thinks you too are worthy of more. Your "more" will look differently than mine, but I love how God is personal in how He approaches each of us in all ways.

I'm not going to for a second pretend that there aren't hurts from misinformed Christians, that there aren't struggles over why a good God "allows" bad things. I'm not able to answer away hard questions. What I hope by sharing something so personal is that you too will believe that you are special, that you are worthy of blessings, and that awful words spoken to you hold no weight so you too may be able to see a picture of yourself that resembles what God sees. You are His princess, worthy to be crowned with nothing but His best.

What Does It Look Like? May 17, 2014

The words *miracle* and *blessings* are mentioned a lot. Some people think they are just warm fuzzy words for good things. Others think they describe what good people are entitled to from God, while some seem to think they are all about what's seen and tangible.

I know I often say I feel so blessed or that I'm waiting on my miracles. Both are true statements and come from a heart that is truly expectant for our babies, knowing that such an event would only be the wonderful work of God with all we've endured and been told on this journey when the day comes. I also feel like there are some things in my life that are God given and do enrich my life, making it a blessing. But I don't just mean the tangible, such as my wonderful babe, the continual encouragement through words in this journey, or the way our section (bare land to build a home) came about. I mean, there's the fact that I have a God who is so real, so personal, who loves me and sustains me, who grows me, who holds me up in the hardships, and who does so much more.

I've been the recipient of gut-wrenching and cruel words, such as, "You don't have babies because of something you've done," "You just don't pray enough or have enough faith," "God promises a prosperous and blessed life, so something's wrong if you are struggling," or "God can work miracles, but you still don't have yours, so clearly He doesn't love you enough."

As these words play like a reel over the years, you begin to believe the words and wonder whether God really is like a wishing well who only grants to the best, who withholds like some bully. You begin to wonder what is so wrong about you that there are struggles and hardships. But as you begin to get into the Word of God and know God's true character and heart, you realize how wrong people are, how you've been led astray, and how damaging that can be.

Please allow me to make something abundantly clear. God is God! He is compassionate, mysterious, sovereign, powerful, and able. The Bible never says being a Christian means you will have an easy life; the opposite is true, in fact. There will be struggles and hardships. This is part of life and the world we live in. But the difference for those of us who know Him and walk with Him is that we don't need to flounder and gasp our way through; we can reach out for His sustaining grace, not just to survive but to thrive.

Something that's always irked me is this prosperity teaching, in which people think material blessings are a given. Rather than thinking the Christian life is about character or growth in God, they think it's all about stuff. This is the lie of "the more stuff you have, the more God is pleased with you." Yes, God gives. Yes, He rewards on earth as well as heaven. But this thinking is getting all out of whack and causing a lot of damage to those who are struggling.

Anyway, once more I digress, and I'm no theologian, so let me leave it there. The reason for this post is that this week in my Bible study, I studied Matthew 7–8. Those familiar with the "ask, seek, knock" and Jesus's early miracles will see my apprehension as I first started. With all the unintended words over the years, it's fair to say that I wasn't overly excited at the prospect of feeling overlooked. All those "Well, if He's able, why don't you have yours yet?" questions posed to me over the years quickly started coming to mind.

However, it's clear to me just what God has been doing over the years, because no condemnation was felt, no "What about me?" or struggles of any kind. Rather the opposite was experienced. I realized that my trust in God has become a firm foundation, and in turn this changes my outlook. What it now looks like to me is that God is indeed able to work miracles and pours out blessings on people. Some are seen, and some are not, and I would go as far as saying that what isn't seen has far more profound effects.

Yes, being able to enjoy being in my home with my babies one day is going to be out of this world—in fact, incredible. The joy felt will be indescribable. However, during this waiting, God has grown me into a person I actually like. Through the hardships He has grown me into a person of character and depth who *knows* Him on a far more significant level. This is a person who will be a far better wife, mother, friend, and support to those on the journey than if this wasn't my reality. So that gives me great assurance when God says He knows best, when He says everything is for our good and not intended to harm us. I now truly believe it and see it.

There are those who are granted quick miracles, others who have to wait a long time, and others who never get one. Only God who is sovereign and mysterious knows the reasons why that is the best for each respective person, and sometimes we need to get to the point that we don't need answers. Our trust in Him is enough.

So if you have weathered a storm, if you are in the throes of hardship and look at what others have and what you don't, will you allow God to change your view from yours to His? Will you dare to trust that He has the best for you and that this trial is part of getting to the plans ahead? If you can't just yet, will you commit to studying His Word and getting to know Him so you can? Are you able to accept that everyone's journey is different? While the grass may look greener on the other side, if you could see the entire picture, you'd probably stick with yours. What does it look like to you now?

Putting Pen to Paper: May 26, 2014

Journaling is a great way to put pen to paper as you process your emotions and struggles. It's a way you can have an outlet and keep a record of the words and promises God has given you, so when you need to be reminded, you can look back. You can see just how far you've come as you look at the pages that are full of snippets of your life, history in the making.

In my mid teen's, when I was going through anorexia and dealing with the first layer of the abuse, I started journaling. I did this for a few years and then no longer needed to. However, in 2008 when our fertility journey was kicking my butt, I once again found myself in need of this outlet.

I remember going from shop to shop in the search of just the right journal. I wanted it to be beautiful, to make me smile each time I picked it up. When the last pages of that journal were filled in 2011, I dragged my feet on purchasing another, as I resented the need and wanted our heartbreaking journey to be over. Finally giving in, I went into the closest stationery shop and purchased the first one I saw. As the final pages of that came to an end this weekend, I took great delight in going to find a new one. It made me smile as I searched for a brand new journal. I realized how the change in attitude over a new journal reflected the different place I was in. The one I found couldn't have been more fitting. It has notes and beautiful flowers, and it just illuminates life, beauty, joy, and new seasons—to me anyway.

I took great delight in writing the final words in the old one and putting it in to archiving, then putting the first entry into the new one. I did love flitting through the pages, seeing God's promises and the way He has had His hand on me all the way through the ups and downs over the many years.

How fitting it is that on Saturday a speaker from America sent this e-mail of God's encouragement:

> Know in this time, and in the trials you are currently finding yourself in, know I am working diligently to position you and to catapult you to your next season.
>
> I am working to launch you into your next phase.
>
> And while it seems hard, and seems weird, and odd, and backwards, know there is a greater purpose being worked within you, and yet to be fully revealed.
>
> For you see parts, and you see pieces, but not all has been shown. So know and trust all this will make more sense to you in seasons and days still yet to come.

I do feel this is a foundation year on all fronts; new seasons are brewing, and while I don't know how things will unfold or in what timing, I know there is reason to sing, to have hope and joy, anticipation and excitement. God is indeed working. So how very fitting that the outside of my new journal will reflect this.

The Persistent Sting: June 18, 2014

Being in such a good space on so many fronts doesn't change the persistent sting of this journey rearing its ugly head unexpectedly, sometimes from seemingly insignificant places. On Friday the phone rang, and once I picked up the call, I realized it wasn't someone I knew. The woman said she had a quick survey, and her first question was "How many school-aged children do you have?" I politely told her we had no children, and that was the end of her wanting my time.

The afternoon went by, and I didn't give the conversation too much more thought. But then as I lay in bed that night, that simple phone call started to niggle at me. I told Brett about it and laughed it off, saying that even in the peace of my own home, I have strangers calling to remind me of my lack and how far outside the normal my existence is. He chuckled along with me and quickly went to sleep. I didn't; my mind kept ticking.

I understand that God is in control, and for reasons beyond me, this reality is the path for us. I still hold onto hope for all the promises given to unfold. I do have that deep peace, that expectant joy and trust that resonate to my inner core that He has us in His hands and that all will be more than okay.

All that doesn't stop there being those persistent stings and moments of struggle, though. I woke on Saturday morning, having forgotten it all, and enjoyed a nice breakfast with my man before he headed out the door to do some work. We were to head to Hamilton that afternoon for my nephew's tenth birthday celebration. Having done all my paper work and various jobs around the house to fill my time, I found myself with spare moments, so I picked up a book. *Slightly Bad Girls of the Bible* by Liz Curtis Higgs had been given to me at the end of the Genesis study, as it had many of those ladies in it. But I'd picked it up just the night before once I finished the last of the many books I'd ordered from Amazon the previous year. On page 12 the words really resonated as such a journey does. I was amazed.

My eyes began to feel the prick of painful tears filling them. I knew the reality of reeling from a bad appointment all too well. I knew what it was like to long for a baby in your arms *now*, to try endless options to see it happen. However, I also knew what it was like to have a word from God and to come back to that at each juncture of desperation. I knew what that faithful endurance brought: people misunderstanding, judging, and causing hurt because they didn't get it. My mind quickly flitted through various snapshots of our own journey, and my heart felt the pangs.

I put the book down and went to the kitchen to get a glass of water, hoping that would snap the emotions. As I stood at the bench, looking out the window at the sky, I knew I could allow myself to fall into the pit of a full-blown pity party. I could turn up to my much-loved nephew's party with a cloud around me that brought others down because of my "lack" and their "have." I could watch on and think about how each of his birthdays reminded me of how our anniversary on the journey was just around the corner. Those thoughts swirled around for a few seconds, and I stomped my foot. No, that wasn't the option I wanted to take. I wouldn't partner with that. "Lord, help me not to be sucked into this pit. Help me instead to focus on Your goodness, on Your promises to us, on what we *do* have, on what is to come and to have a wonderful day, to feel joy for what others are blessed with and celebrate that today."

I sat back down on the couch, curled my legs underneath me, picked up the book, and kept reading. I'm so glad I did, as I found on page 15 a balm for my soul. Before long my man was home, and we had a great time as we traveled down to Hamilton. It was a wonderful time celebrating my nephew, being with family, and watching him enjoy his day.

No matter what journey we face in life, we are constantly confronted with the option to wallow in the bad or enjoy the good. The persistent sting will come, and while we feel it, the choice is ours on how we will deal with it from there. Sometimes we will get it right; other times we won't. But that's okay; it's all part of living life.

The Eye of the Beholder: July 1, 2014

We have all heard the saying that "beauty is in the eye of the beholder," and it's so true. Two people can look at the same person and see such different things. Many class beauty as an outward quality, while some class it as what is within; still others may consider it both outward and inward. Two examples come to mind: There was a girl most people considered a beauty; I saw her and felt intimidated and inadequate, like the ugly duckling. Brett saw her and didn't think she was attractive because of what spilled out from within: the way she treated people and conducted herself. Then there is a lady I know who shocked me one day by saying she was plain and ordinary in appearance. She radiates love and life; there is such a depth in her that shines forth, and when I see her, I see a beautiful lady who loves God, has a heart of gold, and is a joy to be around. It made me feel sad that she felt that way about herself.

But who am I really to talk? You will know from words read that I've not always had great self-esteem or self-confidence. In fact, I'm not sure I'd be as bold as to say I do now. Maybe I will always be a work in progress. I've said some awful things about myself. I've seen such a different picture of me than the God who created and loves me does. Over the years that image has improved, though no matter how comfortable I get in my skin, how much my man adores me or my God grows me, there will be days when I look in the mirror or look at others and think, *If only …*

But what I want to share today has been on my heart, as I've thought of a few moments over the years. So allow me to share those with you first.

In 2008 we were going out to dinner with some friends. We turned up at their place to head off together, only she wasn't ready. As she did the last touches of her makeup, we chatted about our weeks and did the usual chitchat one has. She turned around and told me about a conversation with another friend, one that had stemmed from a magazine, and she posed the same question to me. What beautiful celebrity would I choose if I could look like anyone in the world? She chose Jennifer Aniston. I thought about the question for a moment. Remember that at this point I still had many hung-ups; I was far from the more secure person I am today. But I told her I wasn't sure; if I took on someone else's exterior, I would gain her great points, but I'd also take on her flaws, and I'd trade the parts I loved about myself.

Skip ahead to 2013, when I was at a different friend's house. Her twin girls were playing on the floor, and we were right down there with them, having fun. We chatted about life and what was going on for us both. The conversation came around to the point that neither of us was a fan of our hips, our shape. We both were guilty of saying things like "fatty pie" about ourselves. But she realized that the words that came out of her mouth about herself would shape the way her daughters felt about themselves. We discussed the need for change, for acceptance of ourselves if her children and my "one day" children were ever to have a chance of walking through life less scathed when it came to the worldview of beauty and perfection.

When did everything get so out of control? When did it turn so shallow? Who knows? But the point is, it needs to change.

"I praise you because I am fearfully and wonderfully made; your works are wonderful, I know that full well" (Ps. 139:14).

We need to get to a place that the verse in which God tells each and every one of us that we are *wonderfully* made is an accepted truth. We must not think He did great with those around us but missed the boat when it came to us. He made each of us unique, each of us beautiful and wonderful, with glimpses of perfection and flaws. But even those "flaws" are wonderful, are there on purpose, and are part of the package.

So how can you begin to allow that truth to resonate, to become truth? How will you allow that truth to alter the way you speak about yourself and others? What example are you setting for your loved ones when it comes to their worth, beauty, and acceptance for being their wonderful selves? In what ways can we all flourish and grow if we focus on what God sees and not on what we see?

A Timely Word While in the "Fire": July 10, 2014

I'm sure I can't be the only one who feels God has him or her in a time when their life is about growth and refinement, when He has called us to walk with Him more purposefully. He also wants us to invest into growing in Him on a greater level, all the while knowing God won't leave you to enjoy the transition alone, rather you will be called to share it for other's to be challenged and encouraged. Well, that is where I am.

Until yesterday I was looking through my rose-tinted glasses at this period of life, feeling grateful that God cared enough about me to draw me to Him in a new level, excited and terrified all at once by how my life was changing and all He was doing. It's not an overly comfortable place to be. It's a place of tension; it's wonderful to discover more of Him. It's freeing to grasp certain truths, but it's also uneasy being in the hot seat, where things are being stripped away, where much is given but expected.

All it took was the last straw to break the camel's back, so to speak, and that was yesterday for me, where every aspect of life felt like it had drama. I felt weary and totally unqualified to walk this path, and I even wondered whether maybe just this once God had gotten things wrong when it came to me.

I thought back to 2012, when my Metformin days were over. I was studying Acts in my Bible study and in the process of finishing *A Mum in Waiting*. On a bleak winter's morning, at the end of the Bible study, this dear lady pulled me aside, and we sat down. She had a folded piece of paper and seemed reluctant to share what she was about to. The verse she had was about the refiner's fire, that God would purify me in the fire, that it wouldn't be nice but was needed for what He would unfold from there. I remember getting in the car with the little piece of paper and didn't even enter it into my journal. It wasn't something I wanted to hold onto and see come to fruition. My chat with God went a little something like this as I headed home. *Really? Haven't I been through enough hardship? Haven't my faith and character grown enough that they are acceptable for everyday life? How about using someone else for whatever is to unfold if refining in fire is needed? I wanted ordinary, remember.*

Yesterday, as the wheels fell off the wagon, the Friday in 2012 came to mind, and I knew I was indeed in that period of time. I was in the fire, and it wasn't a great place to be on this particular day. While there had been months of uncomfortable refining and change, they had all been fine because I'd felt God was with me in it all. I was too enthusiastic and happy for certain aspects of "one day" to be too bothered for long. But here I was, feeling flat, tired, and confused.

I got into bed, waiting for the light to go off while my man showered. I decided to pick up my phone. I wanted to check whether there was anything new on my dad, who lives in Indonesia and was in hospital post surgery. But there was no news. I decided to check e-mail on the off chance that a certain e-mail had come in early. You see, some months back a lady had followed my Twitter page. She'd sent me a private message, saying she really felt I should sign up to a prophetic American man's e-mail list, as she felt God would use it for the season I was in. How she knew what season I was in, I didn't know, but I cautiously did as she said. It turned out yet again that God's hand was in it, as his e-mails have been encouraging or challenging at various points.

Anyway I heard that noise to indicate I had e-mail, and there was his e-mail hours early. As I read the words, tears streamed down my checks, my heart tightened, and I thanked God for once again caring so deeply, for being so personal and giving me what I needed in this time of unraveling. I could once again press on. It reminded me that hard work is part of the process, that God was with me and purposefully working in this time of stretching and refinement. I encourage you to press on if you are in such a space too.

Living in an Unnatural State: July 24, 2014

If you looked at my reality, there would be no reason for me to be able to go about my morning. responding to people struggling through IVF, doing business paper work, and then (as I stand folding washing) spontaneously singing, "I sing because I'm happy. I sing because I'm free." with great gusto. But that is the unnatural state I'm currently living in.

Many of you have touched base since you knew that July was marked for us to be doing our third round of IVF. However, many months ago I felt that God said, "Be still and know that I am God" to a deeper level. I struggled to know what that "being still" entailed and to what degree. As those of you who walk a similar journey know, to be able to actively do something helps ease the ache and gives hope. How could I give that up? How could I be sure what God was meaning and asking of me? I grappled with these questions, and my man, who can be so practical and steadfast at times, told me that in the past I've given things to God. Either I was strongly directed, or a door closed, so I should go with that again. I did just that.

I won't lie and say that once I gave the matter to God, asking Him to open or close the door to IVF and help us in whatever was to unfold, that I didn't try at various junctures to wrestle once more and gain control of all the unknowns. But at each of those moments, I once again looked to Him and asked for peace, clarity, and strength to stick to the path He had and not what was natural in me to do.

As July came and we still hadn't heard from the clinic, as one would expect with a plan, I began to struggle again. What if …? There were times when I stared at the phone and longed to pick it up, to tell them to get a hustle on to ensure we weren't overlooked. But then that move isn't being still and waiting on God, is it? So I would again refrain. Then naturally Brett would have waves of wondering what God was doing, saying that while it's my body that would endure IVF, surely it's best to be proactive as this is in our nature; after all, we are coming up to ten years. My heart would break. How I longed to give him peace, to just do it so it eased our reality,

127

knowing it's not just me on this journey. However, I knew from all God had been layering and orchestrating that we were in a season that wasn't natural, that wasn't comfortable. This season required a trust so deep that when the ground shook, I wouldn't be swayed.

Because of this situation, I plunged into reading books, studying the Bible to new levels, listening to godly speakers online, and growing deeper in all God was calling me to. While there are many exciting things He has been doing in such a short space, I don't feel it's the time to share specifics right now. But I can say that from that there has come an incredible sense of freedom. I'm free to be me, exactly who God created me to be. I no longer need to walk a tightrope of trying to fit the mold others have tried to squeeze me into or what my circumstances and brokenness have pushed me to. I am finally excited about what words I have been given and what God seems to be unfolding for the future, rather than trying to scramble away in fear and an overwhelming sense of inadequacy. There is such a sense of joy and freedom in that place.

That place has allowed me to see what isn't yet visible to the eye, to know that there is reason to have faith that our miracles will be fulfilled, that He has got us in the waiting, that His plan will unfold in it's perfect time. This place has allowed me to know that there is reason to have joy, to be free, to know that His eye is on us and that what He has ordained will come to be in all aspects of life.

We neared the end of July with no word from the clinic, and then my cycle began (unusually punctual), and we saw that close the door for sure. What would unfold, I wasn't sure. I am sure there will be sadness as we come upon the ten-year milestone of an unspeakable journey. Yet I am sure that with all God is, with all He is doing, there will still be a reason to be happy, to sing, to feel free, and to flourish in spite of the reality of today, because tomorrow has beautiful unknowns. I can trust my God in the unnatural state He has me in. That I know for sure.

The Joy of Giving: August 1, 2014

Moments leading up to the start of August are always tinged with an ache, a longing, and a deep wondering of when God will change my reality to all He has promised. When has His purpose been worked out to the point that I get to graduate? When can His glory be displayed in its fullness with the miracle that is coming?

With each passing year, that anniversary gets that much harder. As Wednesday, August 27 looms, I see the *tenth* anniversary of a journey I never saw myself walking, let alone waiting for what feels like an eternity. I never expected to see my thirty-fifth birthday looming just behind it without my longed-for and completed family. When will those adorable, grubby-faced miracles puff up their cheeks to help Mummy blow out birthday candles as laughter, smiles, music, fun, and joy fill the air?

I didn't expect this approaching time to be easy. While there certainly is sadness in the waiting, while there is that intensified ache as yet another milestone looms, the song based on Psalm 118:24 softly plays in my mind.

I know that my very faithful God placed that song within me, because I haven't heard it for years. As I stood in the kitchen, going about the task at hand and eagerly awaiting my man to come home, I felt the song pick up momentum. Many thoughts flitted through my head, and then it dawned on me.

This is indeed the day my God has made. He knew before the beginning of times that I would be here in this moment. While it's not an easy place to be, I can still know God has me in it. I know these are the days He has made for me, and there is a purpose and plan within them. I know I can rejoice and be glad in this moment in time, instead of being swallowed up with all the emotions I could be entitled to.

August wasn't going to be a stinker of a month; it was going to be turned around to be a goody. Still more thoughts went through their paces in my mind until it dawned on me that there's nothing that brings me joy like giving. I've been known to give flowers to every staff member in the office on *my* birthday, to shower my family with gifts on *my* celebration. The joy that comes from giving is so much more than if I were the one receiving. So I figured in those moments that it was my day, so why not do what I love to do the most? I've been known to get excited over the smallest of things, such as purchasing two mangoes during groceries and coming home beaming over them. So I knew what unfolded in my mind would be such an amazing blessing for me in August. Now I had something to look forward to: just to have my man arrive home, find the words tumbling out in my excitement, and hear him say yes.

To be expected, my man smiled once I'd gotten it all out and said, "Well, my beautiful, sounds like a good idea, 'cause I know you would love to do the give away." In my whirlwind way, I went about negotiating the budget, sitting down on the couch next to him with pen and paper in hand to decide on the ten items for the ten day give away together. Now, over the coming days I will have the pleasure of purchasing them, wrapping them with pretty ribbons, making cards to go with them, and doing all that fun stuff. Then when August 17 finally comes, the fun can really begin, and I hope *all* of you who live in New Zealand will get behind this ten day give away marking this ten year milestone to make it that much more fun.

Every day from the seventeen till the significant anniversary on the twenty-seventh, to mark our ten years on this journey, there will be a giveaway. In the morning a picture will be put up of what that day's gift is; at the end of the day, a winner will be drawn from those who have entered or were nominated, with names in the comments below the image on Facebook. Then that person will give me an address, so I can get the gift in the mail the next morning, at which time the next gift will be listed.

How fun is that going to be? I'm so excited about it and hope all of you will love the gifts I've come up with—some of my favs, things that have given bright moments, help, or purpose to me through this journey. Now let's try to be patient and see the giveaway unfold as Brett and I decided, for me not to get ahead of myself, like I have on too many other occasions, when I'm bursting with excitement and happiness over something.

Please don't hold back with each day that comes later in the month and get those names streaming in. Thanks in advance for being part of making August such a fun, exciting month, when a stinker is turned into a goody. I so appreciate your participation in advance, as I know you'll love being part of this, and hopefully ten of you will love the gifts that come your way. Oh, I feel like a kid at Christmas. How awesome are my God and my man for allowing me such joy in this moment. This is the day the Lord has made. I will rejoice and be glad in it.

Pressure Cooker: August 11, 2014

You don't need to look very far these days to see unthinkable hardships and tragedies. I don't watch the news because my heart just can't take it anymore. What hits home more, though, is when those we love go through a crisis.

Many of you know that my parents live in Indonesia. I spent a good portion of my growing-up years there. But ten years ago, they returned there. In that time some of the people they serve alongside have become family. A young man, who is considered an honorary son, experienced the unthinkable this weekend. Today is the funeral of his young wife and unborn daughter. To see an image of those two white coffins is heartbreaking and makes this tragedy so very real.

What has moved me to sit and write this morning are the many messages that have streamed in to him. All offer deepest condolences, love, and support. I in no way want to diminish any of that, as it's a beautiful thing to have people pull together and carry one another when the unthinkable strikes. But the common thread between all is "Be strong."

Having experienced pain and loss of a different sort, and in no way even comparable, I know what those words can do. They can create a pressure cooker situation within, where there is an expectation that you grieve for a moment but then pull yourself together in entirety and move on with strength.

The sad reality is that no matter what the hardship is, the rallying in that initial time fades. People go on with their lives, while the one at the core of it all deals with the reality daily, changed forever, with some spoken words playing like a reel. There is power in words.

Over the year I know I have spoken words in love and with the right intent that haven't been taken in the right way. I don't want everyone reading this to beat himself or herself up; we all do. Nor do I want people to think it's better to keep their mouths shut.

However, I do ask that we all think about our words and the implications of them more. I ask people to realize life is short and to put first things first, to make people matter more. Most of all, I'm sitting here writing because I want to reach the hearts of those who may find themselves in that pressure cooker. I want to release the valve for you and say it's okay to struggle, to feel and process. God gets it and allows it. In fact, He holds you in that space. Then He will be the One to put you back together when the time comes for that too.

The Bible is full of people who had faith and strength. But it's also full of people who experienced loss, who didn't always manage through so graciously. The common thread there is that God loves and provides in the ups and downs for those flourishing and floundering.

I know many will want to know how a loving, faithful God can allow the many unthinkable situations in the world we live. I know many want to know the whys to life's big questions. I'm sorry to say I'm not that person to answer them. In my broken times, the only answer I've gotten is that there are mysteries, but they don't alter the character of God. They don't alter the way I've found Him and grown in Him. They don't alter the fact that His grace is sufficient.

You Choose: August 14, 2014

I don't share this to boast of myself, because anyone who has read my book can attest to the broken person I was. I share this testimony to boast of my God; for Him to be able to do the work He has in a girl so broken, so flawed, is incredible. To bring a girl from that place to this, and from this to who knows where, is extraordinary. To do a work so noticeable that I would be able to receive the below message from a friend says it all really.

I share this to remind you that *you* have a choice with the season you find yourself in. You have a choice to ignore God or to run to Him with open arms and allow Him to bring the healing, joy, and the new lease on life; so you can truly discover all He is and how compelling walking with Him is. There is that choice to allow Him to work with the rubble of whatever it is your life has thrown at you, because let's face it: no one has it easy all the time. We're all scarred by one thing or another. No doubt it won't be a childhood of abuse and a ten-year journey of infertility like mine; then again, it could be. But whatever your load is, the same God will take it off your hands and exchange it for a thrilling, new adventure of growth and freedom in Him.

There is no one, and no life, that He can't turn around. Trust me. If He can do what He has in me these past years, then He can do that for you too. There will be pain and aches as the layers are uncovered, but my goodness me, the end result is so worth it. Though I'm sure there will be a continual work-in-progress sign above my head, I know the worst is done, and to get to this point is liberating, to say the least.

Today I got one of those forwarded e-mails from my dear friend, and it truly humbled me and took me aback. But it got me thinking, and I realized that there are some of you out there who need to be encouraged, as you too have made that choice. There are those of you who need to know the choice is there and to get inspired by the possibilities. So read what I have below and allow it to be what it needs to be for you.

"You choose to thrive right where you are. You could be asking for greener ground, for easier choices, for a spot where the sun always shines. And maybe sometimes you do. But you make it through those moments of wishful thinking and you choose to live, to become, to grow in the place where you're planted in this season.

I don't know if you realize how remarkable that choice makes you. In a world of cynicism and discontent, you are rare. And those around you notice. They see your genuine smile and wonder, "Where does that joy come from?" They hear your encouraging words to those around you and ask, "How does she keep her heart open?" They watch you go about your daily life and think, "Maybe there's hope for me too."

So in case no one has told you lately, thank you. Thank you for making the choice to show us all how to bloom and bring beauty, even when life doesn't give us everything we want. Thank you for choosing life, love, and laughter when you could have buried your heart to help you feel safe. Thank you for being a woman whose faith reaches up toward the light of One who loves her.

Your life is a display of his grace. A showing of his love. A reminder of his goodness.

Oh, you may blush and wave that away, thinking that your life is ordinary.

You see the grit, but we see the glory.

And it's extraordinary."

(Original author unknown, but was passed on by my dear friend Barb)

God *Always* Knows Better Than I Do! August 16, 2014

While I know God's timing is perfect, that His ways are higher than mine, and that He always knows better than I, this fact doesn't stop me from imagining and getting ahead of myself at times.

Case in point was my thinking how perfect it would be if I got pregnant with our miracles though my cycle had just occurred. I desired to announce the news at the end of my giveaway and rejoice at the big milestone.

I came to God with great expectations, hopes, and prayers. In boldness I asked that this time may be *the* time. Imagine announcing the news and working out that the date would be April 2015 and getting caught up in all that event would entail.

I even pictured putting a photo from the early scan on my sisters' mattress, as they would be staying on the twenty-seventh for a conference and would be able to scream and share in it all. I anticipated great joy if I could hold out the days till that moment.

However, I also told God that this wasn't a deal breaker for my faith. If it weren't granted, I would still have my deep trust in Him. I would still rejoice in His faithfulness and come to the giveaway and milestone with a joyful heart, continuing to hold onto the promises given and be expectant for one day.

Well, today I awoke to yet another punctual day one. There was a second of disappointment, but then as I shared the news with my wonderful babe, I smiled and said we would just keep trying with each month until it became *the* month. I'm fine because I *know* God's plan and timing are better than mine. He's proved Himself time and again, so I rest in that fact once more. I'm so grateful for a God who carries, provides, and is faithful. I'm so blessed by a man who stands beside me and charges forward with me into all the unknowns.

Today is the day my Lord has made. I will again rejoice and be glad in it. But I have to admit that I can't wait to see what God's version of "perfect timing" is and how it all unfolds from here. Ah, the days that are coming are even better than the current days that are wonderful.

What do your days look like? Are you too waiting for what lies ahead? Will you trust God in the now and enjoy what is? Can you *know* that He always knows best? And if not, will you pursue Him in a way that will see you come to that point?

New Beginnings: August 28, 2014

Yesterday was the ten-year milestone on a journey to become a family, in which some years were filled with unspeakable and awful realities. I remember a time of many tears and unbearable pain, saying, "If God ever saw me reach ten years without my promised miracles, that would be the end of me." I truly thought, when those words were uttered, that reaching such a milestone would be impossible to endure, let alone thrive in.

Well, to the absolute testament of my God, it was the milestone I sailed through because of His work and provision. Since I started getting into His Word in a greater way in 2011, He has graciously been putting the pieces of my life back one bit at a time. This year it has been deep and life-altering pieces. He has done a wonderful miracle that is only from Him—my pre miracle, if you will. That means I could come to August and find there an overwhelming sense of His goodness. While Satan has attacked left, right, and center in every aspect of our lives over these weeks, God hasn't allowed that deep joy and trust to be shaken—in fact, the opposite is true. Each strike has only enlarged my joy, because it reminds me of just what assurances my future holds because of God, the victorious one, the faithful one, the reason for all that is right and good.

Yesterday was the end of my ten-day giveaway to mark this milestone in the theme of my God's provision. Today I want to mark new beginnings. Each of us has walked various roads; each of us is a work in progress at the hand of an ever-mighty and gracious God; each of us has a story to tell and a path to walk. Hopefully through this, you are reminded that if you are in a season that is hard, He has you. Nothing endured is wasted or unending. If you're in a season of triumph, don't hide His radiance but let it flow on to those in need.

When I share, sometimes I forget that no one else sees the words within the sixty-page manuscript of another book God placed on my heart (I started it in July, and it's awaiting its middle and ending). Within those pages the changes are seen, and the new beginnings are grasped. When this year started, we were asked to ponder what studying the book of Matthew meant for us. The words that rang out loud and true were "This is a foundational year." Never in my wildest dreams could I have fathomed what that meant and what God had in store.

Picture, if you will, a bright, pink butterfly with spots of white and stripes of black on it's wings as it emerges from the chrysalis. The wings stretch out as its little legs push off and take flight. That is the image I get when I think of this new beginning that today holds for me.

What Satan intended to use to break me and change my destiny is what God turned around to see His call on my life fulfilled in a deeper way as I was grown, refined, and transformed with a solid foundation in Him built. This may sound wrong to say, but I am humbled and feel privileged that God has allowed me the journey, because out of them He has grown something beyond my wildest dreams. I can't see how I could have one without the other, so I am grateful for all parts but only now that I know my God the way I do. Today I can look back at the many key moments in my life and see how God and Satan were at work, and the hand of my God once again overwhelms me.

I'm beyond excited to see how God unfolds *all* the words and promises we have been given over the years. I am like a child filled with joy and wonder on Christmas eve, with great confidence in what will unfold just around the corner.

May I be so bold as to ask that you allow your season to be all it can be too? You may be in the chrysalis, and the process isn't easy. You may be just emerging as the butterfly, and the journey is possibly a little daunting. You may be that beautiful butterfly that has been flying around for a long time, but you've forgotten that purpose and wonder. Whatever your stage is, will you allow God to challenge and use you? Will you allow those in other seasons to be blessed by where you are? I hope so, as we are not alone in any of this; we all come together to form a beautiful tapestry when we play our part and let God work.

The Power of a Simple Tulip: September 4, 2014

Today I turned thirty-five! It was another milestone I thought would be like the ten year-milestone: crippling. But by the grace of my ever-faithful God, this is my second favorite birthday (my first was as Mrs. Hatton and waking up next to my man).

God never ceases to amaze me, and this birthday was no exception. It started with being at Nosh (an up-market food store), getting some items on Tuesday while I raced around doing errands. I walked in and saw these beautiful pink tulips. They are such happy flowers. You can't help but smile when you see them and appreciate their beauty. I went to pick up a bunch as I thought, *I rarely buy flowers for myself or the house, so why not?* But God said, *Put them back. I have it covered.* I'll admit I had a little pout as I put them back. *But God I want them, and I want them now!*

I went about the rest of the day, having forgotten about them. Come Wednesday I was racing around the house, doing my housework, doing my nails, chatting with my sister, and then heading out the door. A lovely friend from my Bible study had surprised me (knowing it was soon my birthday) and arranged a lunch. On my arriving, one of the dear ladies brought in a gift; it was a crisp white bag, and popping out of the top were beautiful pink tulips.

God knew it was far more special to be gifted something so beautiful and have the reminder that others loved me and that He cares about me so deeply and orchestrates many big and small things in my life to remind me that He's got me. How can that realization not boost my faith for the bigger things I'm still waiting on?

Then on Thursday, my actual birthday arrived. Usually Brett and I spend extra time together, but with it landing on Thursday, I would be at my leaders' Bible study. I felt a little sad that I would miss out on that precious morning start with my wonderful babe, but I was so looking forward to the evening of celebrating together and knew my time with God at the study would be great. However, at five o'clock in the morning a husband who was wide awake woke me an hour before the alarm. He thought I may be awake like usual and keen to hang. A total role reversal. But through it, I got that precious time, and I'm a big quality-time person, so what a gift it was to know that once again God cares and has it all in hand.

When I arrived home from my Bible study, there on my doorstep was a delivery from my dear friend in Sydney. What do you know, but it was another bunch of beautiful flowers—and pink tulips, no less. My eyes pricked with tears. When God says He has it covered, He means it. Again that feeling of knowing others love me and that treasure of knowing God cares so deeply lavished me so greatly and again boosted me to know He's got me in the small and the big aspects of life.

Are you beginning to see a theme here? I am. There are countless ways I've been given a boost, which makes me feel so loved and reminds me that a God who is ever faithful and so very personal deeply loves me.

Just this weekend, after coming so far, being happy to step into the call God seems to have for my life, and longing for Him to unfold it, I had a mini freak-out. I began to question the call, longing to once again retreat but no longer to ordinary life but maybe just to something smaller and a bit different, something that seems more doable. Each day God has been giving me words through devotionals, His Word, my Bible study, and time with my sister over the phone. They have clearly reminded me that those He calls He equips, that it's not about me but about Him. While I allowed all that to digest, He unfolded more.

Through tulips I saw that He cares for me in ways that may seem insignificant but speak loudly. As I unpackaged today's delivery, within me I heard, *See how much I care for you, how I provide for you, even above and beyond. Don't you think that I will do the same with the big things? There is never anything to worry about. I love you. I'm for you. I have you!*

Where could you be struggling to accept or grasp what God has for you? Are you teetering between trust and fear? How will you allow God to speak to you to pull you from teetering to certainty? Maybe a simple tulip could be the moment for profound insight, too. Then again, God is so personal, caring, and creative that I'm sure for you it will be packaged in a way that is unique to you.

Truly Living: September 10, 2014

I dare say that many of us have spent years dulled to the life we are meant to live. We have allowed fears and brokenness to alter the path set before us. Only this year have I allowed God to open my eyes to see that truth and been brave enough to start taking the steps to change my thinking.

God has purposefully created each and every one of us. Our purposes will all look different, but they are all essential. You have been set aside for what God has placed before you. Do you know what that purpose is for you? Are you truly living it out? Or are you holding back out of fear or a sense of inadequacy? Or are you so wrapped up in your world that you are dulled to it? I for one haven't been truly living this purpose out. There has been a mix of reasons.

From a very young age, I had a heart for God. I knew I was unusual in that way because of the sighs, remarks, and looks I'd get because of it. Those responses didn't deter me. However, the abuse, experiences, and lies taken on board through childhood and my teen years dulled that heart. I wanted to know my God and walk with Him. Yet I didn't want to be stirred and grown enough to stand out from the crowd. To me that only brought hurt. I wanted to pull in the person God had created me to be; I wanted to be unnoticed, and I wanted to live a simple and ordinary life. Thus this thinking brought on the years of trying to balance who God had naturally created me to be and who I longed to be instead.

In my teen years and early twenties, I was given words over and over again. They were a bit hard to ignore. But I did my best to stuff them down to be ignored and passed them off as misinformed. Or I tried to reconfigure them to work within what I wanted for my life. I smile now at the thought of telling a Bible study group in 2005, as they all talked about God's purpose for their lives, that mine was to have a strong marriage and family, to grow our business to bless others, and to welcome people into my home and listen and care for them, then send them on their way. I said it would be a simple and ordinary life. I'm not sure whether they bought it, but I did hook, line and sinker.

The theme of these repetitive words continued into my adulthood—that God had a big call on my life, that He had set me apart, that pain endured wouldn't be wasted but used to walk alongside others, and that my marriage and family would impact many. But the theme that scared me beyond belief was being on stage and speaking to others. I could get on board with a few of those events; I could reconfigure them enough to suit my ordinary life but some not so much. *No, Lord, please use someone else.* There was a sense that God had picked the wrong girl, that there would be a million people more suited to such things than I.

I never thought the day would come when He would peel away the layers of fear and lies to the point that He has, so I'm actually excited for the adventures He will unfold and eager to see the spoken words come about to be as He ordains. That deep heart for my compelling, overwhelming, and personal God has returned in full and then some. There's a stirring to truly live and have Him give me the big girl pants needed to be courageous and obedient. That is the natural response when I love and trust my God.

But in that I need to be available. Just yesterday I was dropping off some DVDs to the Ronald McDonald House, and as I walked out, I thought, *Oh, I could volunteer to clean or do nails or something for these wonderful families. I'm already busy, but where there is a will, there is a way.* As I walked to the car, God let me know that while that was noble thinking, I needed to learn not to get so consumed with all that I could do but to invest in what He had for me. For a split second, I once again thought, *But God, don't You think I would be far better at doing such things than what You have for me?* Then I got home and mulled over these three recent verses He'd given me:

> For God's gifts and His call can never be withdrawn.
> (Rom. 11:29)

> I will give you the words I want you to say. (Isa. 51:16)

> Before I formed you in the womb I knew you, I set you apart; I appointed you as a prophet to nations.
> (Jer. 1:5)

The funny thing is that in the work God has been doing over these past months, others are seeing it as well. One lady commented, "It's like you are the Tal we knew and loved but now on steroids." You'll either love it or hate it, but I'm finally happy to be completely me, not the restrained me I unknowingly was. There is something truly freeing about living out who God created and called you to be.

Now don't get me wrong. I don't mean everyone is meant to do what most people think of when they consider "living for God." Thankfully, only a few are called to be missionaries and pastors in the traditional sense of the word. His Word clearly shows us that each of us is called to do something beyond the mundane day-to-day life many of us lead. Only by reading His Word and walking with Him will you unfold the great adventure, purpose, true and full life He has for you.

If you are in the same boat I was, will you ask God to help you truly live? If you are unsure how, why not ask God to reveal His purpose? Or if you know His will but retreat from it, as I did, will you ask Him to give you the courage to step out into it and unfold it all according to His timing?

Let's venture together in truly living. While we are all in our various seasons, they needn't stop us.

I don't just define "truly living" as all of the above. I also think of it as simpler things, such as the following:

- Being confident enough to wear a Pixie Pocket dress because it makes me smile
- Being comfortable enough in my own skin to be the girl who smiles too much, according to some
- Not caring what some will think when the need for a car upgrade comes. Do your husband's dream.
- Leaving tasks for another day so you can seize an unexpected moment with someone who matters
- Forgetting what was and what will be but being fully content and living in the now

So I ask again, will you venture on this road of truly living with me?

God's Gracious Hand: September 13, 2014

Lately, some have asked me questions, and they all lead to the same response. Understandably people can't fathom how I stood in joy at the ten-year mark rather than disintegrating. Nor can they understand why after all this time I still firmly believe God has given me promises and, despite how things may appear, am confident our miracles will come.

How can someone who aches for babies serve children at a Bible study and love it?

They don't understand why our response to a pregnancy announcement or the arrival of babies is to get excited and give a gift. This is my way of saying, "Okay, God, I get it. It's their turn, not mine, and by this response, I want it to be a symbol of blessing them and assuring them I'm okay."

How can someone who endures hardship and waiting continue to think that God is good and faithful? Rather than pulling away from Him, how can he or she grow closer and deeper in relationship with Him?

All these questions lead back to the fact that by the gracious hand of an ever-faithful God, He enables me to do what seems foreign and ill fitting. This seriously isn't me; it's all God.

I wanted to set some of you straight on that. I'm not some rare person who has unbreakable faith and strength or endurance. Nor do I have some deep-seated happiness that never misses a beat. I'm an ordinary girl who has cried many tears, who has come to breaking point and struggled, and whose trust in God has wavered severely.

I just now happen to be an ordinary girl with an extraordinary God who has put the pieces back together to bring healing, restoration, and a newness. By the gracious hand of an ever-faithful God, I am who I am, all because of Him and not because of me. It's because of Him that all the musings of others are made possible. Luke 1:37 says, "For nothing is impossible with God," and I can attest to the truth of that. What seems impossible on our own is made possible with Him.

A dear lady touched base with me after reading *A Mum in Waiting* and said that when she saw my strength and faith, she felt weak. What amazes me is that within the pages of that book, all I can see is brokenness. I don't see the faith and strength others do. So I would suggest something to those of you who are also in that place of great struggle and overwhelming emotions that I have lived and known; it's highly likely that while you see weakness, those around you see tenacity and beauty. Please don't be too hard on yourself. Most importantly, please press into a God who is waiting with open arms to work in a deep and life-changing way for you too.

God loves you so deeply. He longs to know you so intimately and for you to walk with Him and experience all He has for you. There is freedom, wholeness, and joy like you could never fathom when you grow in Him to new levels.

What amazes me is that so many of us have or do settle for less than we should. We believe in God and that He sent His only Son to die on the cross so we may be forgiven and gain eternal life. Some of us even take things a step further than that and start getting to know Him and His ways a little more, becoming involved in church or Bible studies. But we stop short of allowing God to be all He intends to be in our lives, of becoming all we are designed to be.

By the gracious hand of God, all you see in others can be yours too. His gracious hand is waiting to be displayed in your circumstance, in you. That powerful grace is free for the taking if you will just step up, take it, and live it out.

Behind the Scenes: September 15, 2014

Some of you know that I fought God on writing *A Mum in Waiting*. I fought God on doing this blog. I fought God on unfolding the plans He seems to have for me where speaking is concerned.

At each juncture I reminded Him of who I was, of my past, and of how inadequate I was. Surely He would be better off using someone who had it all together, I thought, who was polished, perfect, talented, and gifted to do each thing.

Each request He had for me would put me in a spotlight, so to speak, a place I never wanted to be, a place I had worked hard not to be. I knew who I was and how disappointed people would be when they realized my shortcomings and lacks. They would question my right to be there. I also knew the cost that could come with such a call.

I'm sure many of you are familiar with 2 Corinthians 12.9: "But he said to me, 'My grace is sufficient for you, for my power is made perfect in weakness.'" God uses the weak and broken. He uses what the world would consider castoffs. His power is displayed, and the full glory goes to Him as He uses such people. So I guess in that sense I'm qualified to be called, to be used.

As I've grown in Him, I've learned that those He calls, He equips. It isn't on us to come up with the goods; the burden is entirely on Him. I've also learned that what people connect with is realness, and

I have that in bucket loads. My face is too expressive, my emotions too real not to be genuine.

Recently, with another manuscript under way, because of various blogs that have hit a point with people, or even because of a recent time of my sharing with a group, many have asked how I do it. Okay, get ready for this big reveal ... I pray.

For the very first book and another, I said, *Well, God, I don't have a book in me, so I'll be the fingertips, and You just allow the words You want to be in Your book to flow.* Each time I sit, and my fingers tap; and before you know it, God blows me away with the truths He reveals to me as I read His manuscript or the moments in my life He has put on the pages.

When I feel God prompt something in my heart and know it's time to blog, I again sit before the screen and say, *Well, God, it's time for You to do Your thing again 'cause I'm at a loss as to how to string these stirrings in my heart into words on the screen. Help them to touch those You want to touch through this.*

Then, when God has asked me to speak, there have been times of peace and of freaking out, but regardless, I tell God I agree to be the mouth as long as He does the rest. Obviously I spend time praying and preparing, but I really do just show up and trust Him. There were two times when, as I've approached the mic, I said a quick prayer and asked God to allow His words to flow. And as I stood there, I could hear the muffle of my voice and see the people listening and connecting. But when they came up at the end and said things about what I had shared, I must admit that, while I was deeply encouraged, I had little recollection of what they were responding to. When God uses me as the mouth, it seems like He takes that literally sometimes, 'cause my ears don't function to hear His words.

Picture if you will a spotlight on nothing. That is how I see this. While some of you seem to think it's me, it's not me. I'm merely the fingertips or mouth God uses to reach those He longs to connect with. So while you may wonder how I do it, the steps are simple really: obedience and prayer. God does the rest.

I hope this revelation helps those of you God is stirring to use in a variety of ways; have the assurance that it's about Him. You can bring your real self and feel as inadequate, unable, and weak as you do and still be used by God. He is the One who enables; He is the One who equips those He calls. He is the One who pulls through when you simply obey and trust. When you break the issue down like that, it's not as terrifying, is it? So will you step out and not fight His leading? I fought Him for too long on too many fronts, and now I know the reality of walking with Him as He intended. I see it is a blessing beyond belief. Please don't allow yourself to be cheated out of all God has for you. Instead allow God to unfold it all and see just how wonderful it is to walk with Him in fullness.

(As I read the editors notes at this junction he said that while inspiring it seems my blogs have strayed from being about infertility. And yes, that's right. You'll see a shift in the blogs because of the huge shift in me).

Being on Guard: September 30, 2014

If you've read previous posts, you will have seen that God has been growing me this year. I have felt His unconditional love and freedom that come only from trusting Him in new ways. There has been a shift, as I've been willing to step out and let Him use me, to trust Him to unfold things. Against all odds, there has even been a sense of being content as I lean on Him in this season of waiting. I've experienced joy and happiness, even feeling like I'm floating on cloud nine of late.

I guess you could say I got a bit smug on my cloud. I let my guard down and felt like I was so anchored in God that I was invincible to Satan, to anything he could try through circumstances, others, or whispers. You could say I relaxed in my prayers and spent more of that time praying for others and enjoying my worship time. But last week I got a reality check. There is a reason Ephesians speaks of the armor of God and the importance of putting it on. We are never invincible.

I've been studying Matthew at the in-depth Bible study I go to. As I poured over the lesson of chapters 24–25, I began to feel like I had squandered the gifts God has given me for His purpose, that I had allowed years to be wasted on me and what I had set in motion. Satan began to beat me up with his whispers, and I wondered whether I had indeed missed the boat. Maybe the little I'd been given was wasted so more couldn't be entrusted to me anymore, and perhaps words given were now void.

Then on Wednesday, a day I ordinarily love, I was knocked off my cloud even more. A friend posted an article about sexual abuse on Facebook. As I read it, I made some realizations, both for the good and the bad, as I saw how my experience had played out. I realized there was more pruning to do to be fully set free from the effects. Again those whispers tried to snap me back into emotions and beliefs that were long gone and not mine to bear anymore.

Come Monday, I was in a conversation with someone who made simple statements that left me feeling deflated and reeling. Was the person right? Would it really take God years to grant us our miracles? Did what the person said about questioning the validity of given words hold weight? Was I going to be left out of things and destined for a life that was far from what I'd imagined, with all God had been promising and unfolding?

This morning I woke feeling far from cloud nine. In the midst of the turmoil was still that deep trust, that deep joy, that anchor in my God, that belief in promises given. But there was also a weariness of having listened to lies and whispers, and trying to figure out what was what. I needed to find my bearings again, and that could happen only by turning my eyes to God, silencing all the noises around me, and ensuring that I was on guard and armored up.

So will you find your bearing too if you are in such a spot? Will you allow God to be your anchor? Are you on guard and armored up? If not, will you make sure you make doing so a priority?

Again good old Facebook provided me with something to mull over in light of my week. My sister posted a video of a guy's short inspirational talk; he used a demonstration of a bottle filled with dark liquid, and as he ran it under the tap, the liquid eventually became all clear. He focused on prayer and on how people can feel like it's taking too long and give up, but he said they should keep on because eventually, as you pour in the "clear," the "dark" goes away.

But what resonated for me was that dark liquid; it took a long time to clear. This made me think of how that dark liquid would have been clear and needed only a drop of darkness to permeate it and then need so much clear to make it right again. That picture is what people's words or Satan's whispers can be like in our lives.

If we are on guard, they can quickly be dealt with and discarded, but if we don't and allow them to permeate, to gain momentum not entitled, it takes longer to find that space of clarity, peace, and truth. Being on guard isn't to be taken lightly. So now that I've got my bearings once more, I won't be so relaxed about being on cloud nine, but I will be armored up and on guard so I can remain in that beautiful place with my ever-faithful God. How about you?

Give-and-Take: October 6, 2014

In life there has to be give-and-take. Now don't get me wrong in what I'm about to share; I am a flawed and selfish person. But I find it far easier to give than to receive. In fact, giving—whether it's my time, a listening ear, a word of encouragement, a helping hand, or even a gift—brings me great joy. It's natural to do.

In our early years, Brett had to work on my receiving things from him, especially compliments. Of late God has been working on me to be receptive to what others give. It sounds like this shouldn't be such a struggle, but when one has created a fierce independence due to abuse, it's an element that needs to be chipped away, and the give-and-take is a portion of that process.

I'm trying to be humbler and more gracious to actually receive when it comes, whether it be words, help, or things. Some months back, we had my sister, her husband, and two other couples stay with us during a conference they were here for. Usually when I'm doing a meal and people offer to help, I say I'm good and carry on, but as those words were about to pop out of my mouth, God whispered to me, so I came up with things they could do. Then one of the ladies' husbands was good at just slipping into the kitchen and tidying up afterward, and instead of going in and taking over, I thanked him for his efforts.

Over the months, as God's worked, I've tried to be better at asking when someone could do something for me. I've worked on accepting true friendship, of being open to the give-and-take process. This weekend I had another lesson in receiving.

First off, let me take you back two years, when Brett stumbled across Charlotte from Pixie Pocket in Christchurch (a clothing place that does stunning dresses), when I was disgruntled about summer clothing. She makes beautiful girlie dresses, and I was fortunate enough to have my first dress two Christmases ago. Then for this last one, I purchased two more for some special weddings; then this winter I made more purchases so there were no days in the week without one of these smile-producing dresses. One of my last purchases arrived in the mail this weekend, and I was blown away when inside was a not-so "wee free gift" that I'd been told about. It was a dress; it was simple and elegant. It had material I'd not chosen, but it was perfect. This sweet lady had gotten to know my taste through our dealings and my orders, and for whatever reason (it's still beyond me), she decided to bless me in the most extravagant way. My natural instinct was to thank her profusely but then pay for it, but I withheld from doing the second and am still just so thankful and blown away.

Then yesterday I was in a shop, trying on my new dress with a "cardie" to ensure it worked. As I emerged, some women had entered the shop and were very complimentary about my dress. I actually blushed, but instead of shrinking back and being awkward, I thanked them and accepted their words. My attitude is a work in progress, but I've asked God to help me graciously and humbly accept the variety of giving that is happening so life can truly be give-and-take.

There are so many beautiful people in this world who want to be a blessing, and I don't want to rob them of the joy that is, because I know how incredible it is, so I'm trying to grow in that area.

How about you? Do you need to find a better balance of give-and-take, whichever side you may be leaning heavier on? By God's grace I know it's possible and look forward to getting even better at it, becoming more natural at it and so on.

The Ache: October 13, 2014

As I sit here this morning, once again asking God to pull the variety of emotions and thoughts together into words that will resonate, I remember standing on a small stage at Carey Bible College last year. I had shared the losses and realities of such a journey, but I'd said that in it all I had this sense that God was in control, that He was using this journey; and I felt so humbled by the fact that He'd entrusted this purpose and blessing into our hands.

While I don't think our powerful, loving, and purposeful God initiates much of the hurt in our lives or in this world, I do believe that what Satan intends for harm, God turns around for good. I recall words given to me in my teens, my twenties, and even my thirties that all reiterated that the pain that has been in my life will be used for others. I've seen that truth play out in some ways and know it will continue to do so.

This weekend, emotions mingled as I saw such compassion and an incredible heart ooze from my wonderful man as things unfolded in what the weekend held. We discussed some of what other's were going through and my pride over his response during our drive to Hamilton, realizing that both of our childhoods and this journey had instilled in us characters that could be born only in such hardship. This growth came only from such intense patches. At that moment in time when we were discussing it, I felt grateful, because while there has been much endured, I could also see God's grace and provision through each step of it.

I must admit, as some encounters with amazing children took place later on, that ache within me intensified. A selfishness washed over me as I thought, *God, how about this be someone else's journey and purpose so I may simply live out my dream of motherhood and have older kids with all those memories to cherish now? How about I be at the stage of life I see so many others at?*

On that Saturday night, as I washed my face and cleaned my teeth, my heart thudded with this deep ache and longing for my miracles. I didn't want there to be a wait anymore. I didn't want yet another period to come and signify more waiting. I had this desperate cry within: *Please, God, work Your miracle now. There is a constant desire within, and right now it is heightened. The ache is thudding, and there is pain. I want You to take it away and replace it with the babies I believe you've promised back in 2005 and confirmed over the years again and again.*

As that internal plea went on, I'd moved from the end suite to the room beside it, which had the shelving with my toiletries. Above that is the shelf with all my keepsakes for our miracles, marking many moments in the years gone by. I felt like the day we could use them and have our babies in our arms was so far off as I looked up and surveyed each precious item. Hopping into bed, I read my devotional while my wonderful babe showered. How timely that my reading was about the fact that God hears prayers. Then I snuggled into my man and conveyed some of what was being felt; then my eyes sprang a leak. It turned out that he too had felt many of those emotions with the day's events.

We drifted off to sleep, and as we did, my mind went to a catch-up with a dear lady, who'd asked if I dreamed of holding babies as I slept. I admitted that back in the time of many losses, I regularly had dreams in which I was pregnant and getting to the excitement of sharing only to have intense pain and bleeding. I fully felt the emotions and heaviness in the dreams too. They were more like nightmares that mirrored reality. But no, I'd had no dreams of the blissful state of pregnancy, which was promising, sweet, and wonderful. I'd had no dreams of being a complete family realized. When I daydreamed of "one day" or painted pictures of hope for us, they never entailed pregnancies, announcements, births, or babies. While I knew the day would come, as promised, with all that had been endured, it felt too impossible to dream of, like an aloof pot of gold at the end of the rainbow. Instead, my painted pictures of hope were of toddlers racing around the home, being delightful and cheeky, the home full of love and laughter. The night before was my first dream of holding a baby in our arms, but there was only one, and the experience ended in tragedy. That night I tossed and turned, but there was no dream.

The following day we were at a fund-raising concert, and in front of us was the picture of perfection: a cool young couple with an adorable toddler and baby. They looked so happy. I caught myself looking at them with a smile at times, thinking of one day; all the while the thud and ache intensified. *Why God? When God? How God? … So many questions, longings, and feelings. I'm so very far from the woman of faith, peace, joy, and contentment I'd felt like not too long ago.*

That night, as I drifted to sleep, I dreamed this time of being a driver for some kids' outing, many of whom I knew and loved. The comments I get all too often came in the dream too. "Which is your child? Oh really, but you are such a natural. Seems such a waste." As I walked along a path, a sweet mother and child I didn't know asked me to stop. The little girl said, "God wants you to know He loves you, and I can see you are going to be such a good mamma one day."

In the dream, tears flowed as I smiled and said, "Thank you" before making a quick exit to sob.

As I did, the mum asked her daughter what that was about, and she said, "God told me her heart was sore and she needed to remember important things." Then I woke with this mixed feeling of sadness and longing, along with wonder at how graciously God inserts reminders of Himself amid dips in the road.

How timely then that this morning I pulled out my in-depth Bible study homework to review, now that the holidays are over, for what lies ahead. I saw question six, which asks, "What has God entrusted to you that He would like you to 'invest' or use?" The answer I wrote weeks back, as I look over it today in this place of disgruntled ache, is a timely reminder to me: "I have walked painful and hard paths but experienced God's love, freedom, and joy that I may stand and speak of a God who longs to do the same in the broken people He has me walk alongside, that they too may have hope, faith, and all God will unfold as I'm used."

That's right. Pick myself up yet again, dust myself off once more, stand on truths that are unshakeable, and focus my eyes on the One and keep on keeping on. From the moment I was a twinkling in my parents' eyes, God knew me. He had called me by name; I was His. I had been created with my attributes and flaws for a purpose that was mine alone to walk. The road may feel hard and long at times. I may experience dips in it, but the truth remains … God's hand is on me, His provision is constant, and His promises, given and reassured in my times of need, stand. I may not always feel like it, but there are blessings to be found in the midst of all this and hope for what is to come. The list goes on and on of all the wonderful truths there are when I focus my eyes on my God and His ways.

The Bible gives stories of many to whom God gave purposes and promises. They were considered women and men of great faith, but you will see the peaks and valleys in their roads. We may not see ourselves anywhere near their realm, but don't forget that each of us has a God-given purpose to walk out. Each of us is considered many wonderful things in the sight of our very real and personal God. So whether we currently find ourselves on a peak or in a valley, please may we all remember that God has us and that we can call on Him as we walk, grow, and develop. We are free to be real with Him in every sense of the word.

Something I've realized today is that my valleys often come when the in-depth Bible study I go to is on a break, because I'm not immersed in His Word the same. I don't find the balm to my ache by serving with children and being among friends who sharpen me.

That is a tendency I need to be aware of and counter, especially with this three-month break coming up at the end of next month.

So how about you? Are you aware of issues that may cause dips in the road? How will you counter them?

God Does Speak: October 15, 2014

I'll admit that sometimes I feel guilty that in our journey God has given us promises for our miracles, because this fact certainly makes it an easier road to walk. Sometimes as I listen to women share of their journey and that longing to know what will unfold and what the purpose of all this heartache is, I wish I could give them something to ease it. At such times I ask God for a word for them, or I ask Him why we have been given a promise, while others are left uncertain.

We all know that life is complex, and it's far from a cookie-cutter life. The reason for one person's road isn't the same for others. The reason for someone getting words from God while other's struggle in silence is varied too. But I think sometimes we can look or listen in one place and not notice that He is indeed there and speaking, just not as expected. God can't be put in a box; He isn't limited, so we need to be more open and aware.

Something I've realized in the week after aching is this: I was feeling like God was further away than normal, and I didn't like that. However, the reason was me. He wasn't further away; I just wasn't taking in all that I had been. I felt flat, so I didn't open the Word of God as I usually would have. I felt despondent and didn't find the motivation to pick up a book to keep gleaning from it. I didn't keep my eyes wide open and missed the rainbows in the sky or the rays of light beaming through the clouds, which is the way God usually reminds me He is there. I had allowed tiredness to take over, so I didn't find the motivation or time to spend praying and listening, to truly allow the music that would ordinarily stir my heart to worship, or to even listen to godly speakers while prepping meals, as once had been normal. I was the block and distance where God was concerned; the issue wasn't Him. As I realized all this and again felt a pang over someone else's struggle when I compared it to mine, a few pennies dropped, so to speak.

Sometimes we don't hear God because we don't bother speaking with Him. In 2005, when God gave me the first promise for our miracles (again in 2006, and then it was added to me in 2010, 2013, and 2014, when it was confirmed and expanded yet again), there had been a desperate and unrelenting cry to God for answers. I was bold in what I asked for. I was specific in what I needed to know and was open to what was then given.

We can sometimes ask but not listen. It seems like a crazy notion, but it can be the case. I've done that before. I sat on the couch, having talked to God about things, and then I didn't feel like He was working quickly enough for me, so I picked up my phone, switched on the TV, got the laptop, or did paper work or one of many options for our fast-paced lives. God uses many ways to speak to us, and if we rush through life, we miss them. For example, sometimes I read my devotional and realize I'm simply going through the motions in my haste to get through my big to-do list, and the devotional became part of the rush instead of what it should be. I realize, reprioritize, and read it again and am amazed at how God used it to speak to me in the way I'd asked for. But I'd almost missed that. How often do we do that?

Other times I think we do hear from God but choose to consider His message as unacceptable, so instead we cross our arms, stomp our feet, and let out a huff. I know I've done that. I didn't want to be told to trust in Him and wait on His timing, because I thought His timing was too long. I didn't want to be told that the plans He had for my life were so different compared to what I had laid out.

Then there is fear. In 2005 it took a while for me to be brave enough to ask Him for an answer on whether we would be parents. I was terrified the answer may be no. I was scared that I would then struggle to understand why He had planted such a clear desire in us for family and created various aspects to our beings and marriage if His answer was a no, so the unknown felt more workable.

If I'm honest, I think there can also be times when God knows we're not ready for an answer, for an unfolding of God-ordained plans, so He just sits on it till we are. Once I finally got on board with God's using me to speak, I wanted to get started and was frustrated when there were no opportunities. I even wondered whether I'd missed the boat and was deemed unusable because of my refusing His plan for twenty-years and doing my own thing. But then I realized that there are seasons for all things; they don't negate the truth of answers or words. They don't mean God has deactivated them, just that they are on hold for now for a reason only He knows.

Maybe you're above all these issues, and it's just me who is the slow learner. But on the off chance it's not and you are in a place where you read of others hearing from God or are given words and sit there, thinking, *But what about me?* Then can I suggest you get talking, listening, and accepting? I'll work on those too. I guess the process is always a work in progress, like any relationship; it has to be ongoing.

Love Is …: October 16, 2014

If you have read my blogs or book, you will have seen that I'm blessed with the most incredible husband and that we share a very special marriage. Many joke and ask, "Does he have a brother?" I don't take it for granted for one second how deeply blessed I am on that front.

I won't pretend that there haven't been hard times over the years. I won't for a minute say there isn't work required. But I find myself sitting here and writing about my view of love, because I think many forget what true love is, what it requires, and that it's not just for a select few.

Allow me to take you back some years; for some this portion will be known, but I do so for those newly on board. At a young age, what I wanted most in life was to be an amazing wife and mum. Then abuse came and altered that longing.

My history with boys on the dating front is very simplistic. During my high school years, I had a "boyfriend" for a few days. We talked on the phone once, and then I heard that he wanted to kiss me at lunch, and I went over to end it. A few years later, I was in Australia, and there was a boy and mutual attraction, but when he showed interest by trying to hold my hand, that was the end of that. Then I had a "boyfriend" for a week, which started long distance from a well-established friendship, but as soon as we saw each other at church and he went to hug me, I once again ended it.

I'm sure you can gather from that that because of my past abuse, I was adverse to physical contact of any sort, and I was very quick to put up a wall and keep to myself. At the age of sixteen, when I'd decided my life would consist of God and me, someone gave me a book, saying the gift was from God's prompting. The book was about dating, sex, singleness, and marriage. I didn't see how the book was relevant to me, but I read it anyway. By the end I knew in my heart that God had marriage on the table for me and that I was to commit to praying daily for the person God had for me, for myself, for our marriage, and for all that good stuff.

In the day and age we lived in, I was scoffed at when I shared that part of my prayer was that God would set my future husband aside in every sense of the word and that we would be each other's first kiss, and waiting for marriage for sex. I prayed that God would prepare us in character for one another and that our marriage would be concrete and set apart, along with many other values that were important to me.

At the age of seventeen, when I was at yet another new youth group, I had an ordeal on the Saturday night that left me ragged. I had flashbacks to abuse and had to deal with hard emotions. I was mortified that these new people who hadn't gotten to know me well enough yet saw a side that held such pain, damage, and shame. I went to church the following day with my head low, wishing it was time to move on yet again (with growing up as a missionary kid and a stint with them being pastors we moved a lot). Instead there was a guest speaker, and at the end, he and his wife prayed for me.

Many significant things were said and prayed that day. But what was relevant was that I was told that God had a future husband set aside for me and that he would adore me, cherish me, and be besotted with me. He would treat me in a way I could never imagine; there was no need to fear that he would hurt me in the ways I expected. It would be a special marriage, one that would impact many just by being.

I went home, writing the experience down to look back on but not thinking it was possible, even for God. It turned out that this special someone was Brett, the amazing guy I'd become friends with at youth group. I'd love to say that from there everything just fell into place and was perfection, but I can't.

As seems to be the case with most newbies, there is interest, so one night in the youth group van, I set everyone straight; I wasn't interested in boyfriends for the sake of having one. I was waiting for that special someone I believed God had promised, so please let's just be friends and leave the silliness out. For some reason, this didn't deter Brett. He liked me, and when I found this out, in true fashion given my damaged self, I retreated. Months later we started hanging out in the same group again, and a real friendship blossomed.

One night in June 1998, we were all at an older youth group person's twenty-first birthday. As I walked across the room and made my way to friends, I saw Brett, and my heart fluttered. Then God told me he was the person I would marry. I remember leaving that night and looking out the car window at the dark night and bright lights, talking to God about what had unfolded. I started praying intentionally about His message. To my disappointment, some months later, Brett started going out with someone else, so I changed my prayers. However, when God sets aside two people and has a plan and purpose, no matter what, God unfolds it to be as He ordained.

That November Brett was again single; we started spending a lot of time together in a smaller group, and come the beginning of December, I plucked up the courage to say I liked him as more than a friend. It turned out that he still felt the same way but was reluctant to say so, as he'd been burned before. But I told him that I still wasn't going to be with someone for the sake of it. I felt that he was the one for me and that I wanted him to take time to think about it and pray about it before we took the next step. To my surprise, he didn't run for the hills. (I drafted this blog and asked him to read it to ensure he was happy with it and so he could get a glimpse of how I view him, only to find, all these years after that conversation, that all he heard in that big chat all those years ago was "She's into me, yes!" So I guess that's why he didn't run for the hills. It worked out well for me, though.)

On December 7, 1998, Brett and I started going out. Our relationship was official, and I was so incredibly happy. Three months into it, he told his group of guys that he knew I was the one he was going to marry; he couldn't explain it, but he just knew. I think our close friends thought we were crazy being so young and "knowing" such a big thing. Sadly, the relationship wasn't all smooth sailing; eighteen months in, issues were hard. There were big fights because of my insecurities from abuse, his anger from his father's death, and all that this encompassed, so combining those matters created great issues. Friends told us to break up. Our parents told us to end it. Even our youth pastor called me into his office and gave me an ultimatum.

We both stood our ground because we knew beyond a shadow of doubt that we were each other's person, that breaking up wouldn't resolve the problem, and that we needed to instead work on fixing the root of the issues. In my early twenties, I went to counseling to start working on some of the patterns of beliefs that came from the abuse in my past. That helped a lot but still didn't solve it all. After a trip away with his best mate, Brett came back and said we needed a week to think about our future on our own; then we would decide at the end where to go from here. I felt sick as each day passed. I couldn't sleep or eat; I was terrified that he would decide to walk away from me. On Thursday the phone rang, and it was him, three days early. He wanted to meet up to talk, if I was clear on what I wanted too. I said yes and numbly drove to his place, my stomach turning, convinced I was about to be on the receiving end of heartache. All I could do was pray and leave the matter to God.

I sat across from him and couldn't believe my ears as I listened to the words tumble out of his mouth. He loved me. He believed we were each other's person and that our future held marriage. He would work on his anger from that day forward, and things would be different, and I would continue working on my issues from the abuse. We would work together on our relationship, and when things had been good for a year and he had finished his building apprenticeship, we would get engaged. That day was indeed our turning point.

On February 1, 2003, we were married, and words those around us spoke on that day were a reflection of the work God had done in bringing two people together. The days that followed were amazing. I loved waking up next to my wonderful man each day, and still to this day that wonder and appreciation haven't worn off. He still makes my heart flutter.

Living in the house we'd built and had our first night of married life in was amazing. There was so much fun as we set up house and as we grew up together and enjoyed all that married life held.

We made decisions together. We respected one another. We chose to love each and every day. We communicated in the big and small things. We compromised and ensured there was give-and-take. We put each other first and were considerate and selfless in our approach. The aim was always about making the other person happy, lifting his or her load, and making the person feel loved. We would be creative and go the extra mile in our ways to deliver those goals. We kept the foundation of our values and traditional ways, because that is what worked for us.

Don't get me wrong; all that wasn't always easy. The realities of infertility mounted. The recession hit business and our finances hard. Outside factors caused friction, and we again had to make that conscious decision and effort to come back to what our marriage was about and invest into it all those qualities that made it so special, that saw it be what God said it would be.

When I look back and think on what God promised for my marriage, I can attest to all that being fulfilled and then some. Never in my wildest dreams could I have imagined being adored and loved the way I am, being able to look into my wonderful man's eyes, seeing the outpouring of all he feels for me, feeling the touch of his hand on my back, and knowing what security and faithfulness come with that hand. I love hearing the beat of his heart as my head rests on his chest and being assured that his heart beats for me and one day for our children.

His character exudes many qualities I admire greatly, ones I've seen born out of adversity and hardship. But that's what makes them worth their weight, for those characteristics are rock solid and unchanging. They weren't born in a fleeting moment but were shaped and chiseled over time. Each crease around his eye has been placed there with me by his side; I know that some of those creases represent the times we've laughed and enjoyed adventures, but others are from when he's gone to the edge of the cliff and stared down into the darkness by my side.

On the day I spoke at Carey Bible College last year, what resonated with me the most was about my husband. After all I shared about the journey, someone asked me at the end, "What will we get with reading your book?"

My response was "You will see a powerful God, a loving husband, and a broken me." At the end a few guys came up and said that what they got out of it the most was what love looks like. You see, all too often people forget what love is in a world that is filled with me, me, me.

I can understand how impressive it is to hear of a husband who goes to bat for his wife when the going gets tough, sleeps on hospital floors and armchairs to remain by my side, passes ice chips and heat packs during treatments, rubs backs when there is physical pain, and holds me tight when there's internal pain. He is a man who does more than his share around the home when the realities of infertility in one way take me out of action; he knows just what to say or when to say nothing and so much more. It's sad that nowadays people are amazed when a husband doesn't walk away but remains when inconceivable hardship is endured and for so long. That is when they see what love is and how tenacious and selfless it needs to be.

In jest people say the way Brett gets up to clean up dishes of his own accord gives others a bad reputation. When he gives me a compliment or displays consideration, there is a dig in the side of another husband by his wife. It goes the other way too; when I do something for Brett, something others consider grand or even simple but thoughtful, there is a dig in the other direction. Now I'm going to get really honest here, and hopefully I don't offend anyone, but do you know what I see with that? I see two people who want the benefits of what Brett and I share but don't want to put in the effort it takes. The truth is, if others truly want that kind of marriage, that type of love, then they could have it. I shared the beginning of our story to show you it wasn't always smooth sailing; we could have given up or allowed it to stay with baggage and bad patterns. But we didn't. By God's grace, as teens having looked on at others marriages and not seeing what we wanted but rather an example of what we didn't want, we worked our way through difficulty to find how to truly love each other and build a marriage that is indeed all God promised.

I don't know what it is about our marriage that makes strangers in a store comment on it or friends and family say all they do, because truth be told, I don't know how the simple daily interactions can paint such a picture to the outside world of what happens behind the walls of our home. But I know from being on the inside of it that a marriage takes a choice each day; it takes work that has now become like an effortless, well-oiled machine with the slight glitch from time to time.

Did you know that for years, when my man would arrive home and I'd hear the garage door go up, I would race down the hall like an excited puppy and open the internal garage door with a big grin to welcome him home? I didn't realize how much my excitement of his return home meant to him; he felt wanted, loved, and welcomed. It wasn't until the end of my being on Metformin for fifteen months (in much of his home time, he would see me bedridden, so I wouldn't do what had been usual for eight years) that I discovered how much that simple event meant to him. Now I make the effort to be home to give him the welcome home or drop whatever I may be doing so that simple gesture paints the picture of just how important he is to me. I love knowing that, after all these years, he turns that corner, and his heart races, knowing his wife will be there with a beaming face to welcome him home.

Love is simple, selfless, considerate, and powerful. It makes a huge difference. Please don't just see the love I have for my man within my words or give him props for all he does but allow my words to go beyond that.

Take note of the way your husband or wife loves you and appreciate it.

Take note of the way your husband or wife needs your love shown and do it.

Those two simple steps will unfold a reality that you too are loved greatly, that you have the capacity to return that love greatly too. Love is what you make of it.

The Beauty in Iron: October 28, 2014

The other weekend Brett and I traveled the East Cape roads to get some much-needed time out together. On the stunning drive, we were again reminded of the beauty in this world God had created, of the importance in taking quality time and so much more.

Our first night started in Ohope, and the guy at the hotel where we stayed was so genuine. He gave us great information on what the must-hit spots on our journey were, and we just had a good yarn. The next day, while driving on the back roads toward the lighthouse, we came across an older woman traveling alone. We struck up a conversation and encouraged her that she couldn't just do the drive and not walk the seven hundred steps to the top, that she could join us to have company. And so began a lovely and insightful time. As we headed back to the main road, I reflected on how those two interactions left an impression, and if we had done what seems to be the way in today's fast-paced life, we would have missed such moments. You just never know the life lived or experiences had unless you take the time to interact with others. This event made me realize that through our experiences, people matter, and because we take the time for such interactions, something wonderful can come of them. I felt grateful for that, another plus to such hard roads.

The following night I sat across from my man over a nice dinner out in Hastings, and the conversation led him to say that he wouldn't trade the last ten years for anything, because they've made us who we are. They've shaped what our lives are. They've given us experiences and connections that wouldn't be there otherwise. While we yearn for our miracles, we see that these ten years have created something special that wouldn't have been there otherwise on many fronts. How fitting then that the next day, as we looked through yet another home store, we found the antique iron I had been wanting for some time. I purchased it, and when we finally get to build on the land we'd purchased last year, I will be able to display it on my bookshelf and have it as the reminder I want.

"As iron sharpens iron, so a friend sharpens a friend" (Prov. 27:17).

Life is filled with moments that refine you, that grow you and unfold a purpose beyond your wildest dream. God has placed people in my life throughout the years who have sharpened me as iron would, and there is great beauty in that. Sharpening may not always feel nice, but it is essential, and you can be blessed with people who love you enough to invest in you in such a way that they need to be appreciated and utilized.

Let me share with you two such moments when I was sharpened. One was in 2007, when we were going through the intense process of my being diagnosed with endometriosis, and my first surgery was looming. We had been battling with the insurance company over it, and it was fair to say that emotions were heightened, and I felt much like a punching bag. Brett and I were in the supermarket, grabbing a few things on a weekend, and the place was chaos. There were screaming children, ignorant people were taking up all the space without a care in the world for those around them, the stock was low, and the staff were frazzled.

We stood at the chicken section, and it was carnage. I called out nicely to a young guy with his supermarket uniform on, but when he came over and wasn't the most on-to-it person, my niceness disappeared, and frustration and rudeness replaced it. How hard was it to answer a simple question? His inability left me fuming and was the final straw. But as we walked away, I was reprimanded like a child, treatment I wasn't a fan of, so I tried to defend myself. Brett had a point, though; just because our life was in upheaval, the supermarket was in chaos, and the other person didn't conduct themselves in a way one should expect, that didn't give me any right to speak sharply to another person. In that moment I was sharpened as iron would be; my husband cared enough about my character to have an uncomfortable moment. To this day the moment has stuck with me.

Then in 2013 God stirred me through the in-depth Bible study, and I knew He was in the process of growing me to use me. In obedience I went along to a homiletics seminar, though if I'm honest, I was dragging my feet in defiance, spouting off all kinds of "Well, you can do this, but that is off limits." As I sat down with my pen and paper ready, the lady leading it said some words that set my heart racing. I wish I could remember her exact words; they were something about some being there because God had ordained it, that this would be a tool for His purposes in time to come. I knew in my spirit that that someone was me, and her words made me mad. Hadn't God listened to my stipulations? Afterward the lady came up to me and said that in all the years, she'd never opened with those words, that she'd gotten chills from them, and that she was confident they were about me.

As Joan and I stood in the kitchen, God brought to memory words spoken to me at age seventeen, words I'd suppressed, and as I looked at her, I knew she would be instrumental in the foundational years to what God would unfold from there. I'll admit that my independence born from pain made me rather un-teachable and defiant, so God had His work cut out in using her. But over the months, what He unfolded indeed made her someone who was able to get past the layers and teach me, to invest in me, and to see God's plans and purposes unfold. Even to this day, she continues to sharpen me, and sometimes I react in an ungracious way. But once I go away and mull her words over, I know she's right, though I'm sure she has no idea how instrumental she is in what God is doing with me.

I love that God cares more about our character than our comfort. I love that He brings people across our paths who love us enough to invest in us, sharpen us, and see coal turned into diamonds over time. My nugget of coal still has a long way to go, but I know the process is under way, and one day God will be able to say, "Well done, my good and faithful servant. At last, Tal, you let go and let me, and look at the result."

How do you fare in this whole process? Are you one of those special people who sharpen others and see the results of God's work through you? If so, I commend and thank you. Or are you on my side of things and the one being sharpened? How receptive are you to the process? Will you see the beauty in the ironing process? Will you appreciate the iron and the Creator? Won't you try to surrender to the process with me?

Not Overlooked: November 3, 2014

If you have been journeying with me, you will know that God has been working on me and growing me. Sometimes the blogs may portray a picture of a girl who is so valiant and strong in her faith. Other times they portray someone struggling and wrestling, possibly someone whom many would write off. I have no doubt that as some of you read this latest blog, you will shake your head a little. When, oh when, will I stop having this internal tug-of-war? When will I finally grasp how big my God is and what He has purposed for me? The simple answer is, I don't know. I am a work in progress, and I'm actually okay with that.

I'm coming up on a year and a half that I will have been serving as a children's leader for the in-depth Bible study I go to. I still remember the weeks leading up to that event, as if they were yesterday. As God was growing me, I was being stirred out of the box I had placed around my existence. He clearly told me that I was being shifted into serving Him and that my days were no longer going to be my own. Never in a million years would I have concluded that events would unfold as they did. In fact, if I'm brutally honest, I felt like serving in kid's was a death sentence, the death of a dream for my own miracles, the death of words prophesied. I thought I was being stuck down in the dungeon to be forgotten. But I couldn't deny that God very clearly told me my answer should be yes, and how could I not be obedient when my God had once again become such a deep part of my life? Surely with all I had learned about His character, I could trust Him that my perceived "death sentence" was anything but.

That year was the study of Matthew, and at the beginning God told me it would be a foundational year for me. By then I saw how greatly God knew me better than I did myself. I saw how He brought such joy into my world with being a kids' leader. I could attest to how faithful He was and how what He purposed and unfolded was far better than anything I could have possibly hoped or dreamed for (though I'll admit that hasn't stopped a few tantrums over still waiting on things; patience just isn't my thing).

As the year progressed, I can see how indeed it was a foundational year on so many fronts. After twenty-nine years of believing in Jesus as Lord and Savior, I have finally grasped and accepted the grace and unconditional love that comes with salvation. I have found healing, restoration, freedom, depth, and so much more than I knew was mine for the taking. Grasping the depth of God's love for me has been life changing. Through the acceptance of His grace and love for *me* He has created in me a yearning for more of Him and a heart to share this desire with others.

If I'm honest with the words given since my teens and my newfound heart, I once again boxed God in and concluded how things would unfold. I saw me sharing my testimony a few times a year in various places and that being how the words for my future was fulfilled. I got comfortable in thinking that was how my life would play out one day, though I was itching for my speaking on that format to start. I loved my role at the in-depth Bible study and felt settled and was in for the long haul.

However, God never allows me to stay in such mind-sets for very long. Over the past month, He has been stirring me, telling me that I can't get comfortable and think what I have is for the long term. He gently reminds me that there are stepping-stones, and I'm only at the beginning. We have been told that He has adventures for us after all. (Again in these moments, I forget that you guys haven't read the manuscript for the next book, so I do apologize in advance for thinking you get things you may not.) That didn't stop me from balking at something I was asked to prayerfully consider though. *Really, God, come on. Have You forgotten who You are working with here?*

Just last week, there was to be a seminar on Friday about quiet times. I had no intention of going, because I love my times with God and figure I have them down pat. Also October had been a full month, and I had things to do, so any time I could grab was worthwhile. God asked, *Tal, are you that arrogant that you can't give Me two hours to attend this and learn more ways of being with Me?*

Okay, God, You have it. I'll go. So I did.

As I sat there, learning, I was grateful. The exercise spoke to me greatly because I'd had a week of thinking something was absurd. I wasn't smart. I wasn't articulate. I wasn't learned. I wasn't together, godly, and able. In fact, as I sat in that seminar, I was between two woman who were learned and capable, and as I sat writing in my notebook, I felt stupid. I wasn't sure how to spell some words. *See, God, I can't do what You may be asking of me.*

I remember that teachers in school were frustrated with me. They wrote in my report that I was smart; if only I would apply myself, the world was my oyster. My parents came back from parent-teacher interviews and said the same thing had been reiterated. Having recognition for a few things, I shrank back; mediocrity was what I wanted then. Getting attention hadn't served me well in the past, or so I'd thought. Now I regretted allowing my brain to go to mush.

I only have authority on my own life to be able to stand on some stages to share a testimony. I can't mess that up, 'cause I lived it. But by the time I got to the end of the seminar, there was excitement bubbling up within. God used the unlearned; He taught people just like me so we weren't overlooked.

While I have no clue what God will unfold from here, I do know that my past doesn't determine my future. I am so very grateful for that, because there is a yearning in me for more than what I boxed myself into. I want more. Hopefully, as God unfolds each stepping-stone, I won't fight it so much. Maybe I will trust and be obedient quicker. Time will tell.

How about you? Are you yearning for more? Have you boxed yourself in? Is your past determining your future? Have you written yourself off when God is only just getting started? Will you please allow Him to change all those hang-ups so you don't miss out on what He's ordained?

Disorderly and Uncomfortable: November 26, 2014

If you looked inside my home, you would see that I like to have things orderly. By peeking into the cupboards in any room, you would be able to piece together a picture of my personality and how I like to do life. But as has been well established, life plans don't always unfold as we set out. All too often life throws curve balls, and in those there is a choice to be made, for the positive or negative.

Never in all my hoping, praying, and imagining what life would be could I have pictured what it is. For someone who likes to have things set out in a logical, clear, and orderly fashion, you would think the realities would unravel me.

Of late there have been some interesting conversations with an array of friends, and those have had me pondering many things. All the pondering leads me to stand back in awe of the God I know and walk with.

What never ceases to amaze me is how complex my life has been, how mixed my personality is, and, as a result, how things have unfolded as I submit my ways to God and am willing to grow in Him to walk the paths of unknowns and adventures.

The in-depth Bible study has wound up for the year, and as I think back over the study of Matthew and how God told me this would be a foundational year, I am blown away by what that actually means. It's been a year of some huge shifts in accepting some foundational truths in my faith on who God has created me to be and the purposes He seems to have for us. There is such freedom in all that, but with it also comes the need to stand firm in what is disorderly and uncomfortable.

Yes, there have been huge losses on many fronts on that road of infertility. Even still, when I think back on certain points, there are tears at just what was endured and disbelief that it was experienced. However, there have also been huge gains, big growth, and required change—none of which could have happened without the other.

While another Christmas looms and many milestones highlight the gaping want in our lives, I'm still standing firm in what I shared and felt in July. Some of you will remember that we were scheduled for another round of IVF in July, but things unfolded for that not to happen. The clinic didn't contact us, and my feeling was that we were to wait on God. Brett supported me in that decision.

Naturally, it would have been nice if the long-awaited promised miracles had come about between that hard decision and now. How nice it would have been to triumphantly share the news and have people see God's faithfulness and ways, and for there to be haste with it, to see it was worth following His prompting and not faltering. What a double miracle it would have been to have tried all we did and then to be able to avoid more horrific treatments and losses, with the pregnancy happening naturally. Instead we are asked on a regular basis about where things are, and many are perplexed with us for not chasing the clinic and pushing things into being. The judgment of some shines through in their responses, both spoken and unspoken.

If I'm honest, I'll admit that it's a very uncomfortable position to be in. I know beyond a shadow of doubt that God has closed that door and has us waiting. I have no clue what He will unfold from here or what His timing is. I've learned over this journey that no amount of trying to figure it out will result in knowing. While there is still that ache for my babies, there is a contentedness, a deep joy, and an unwavering hope, for I know my God has *all* things covered.

Some weeks back, I said to Brett that I felt I was viewed as a fool. It's been over ten years, and yet I still have great expectation and certainty that the promised babies will come to fruition. It's been months of waiting, and yet I am still content for God, not people, to lead me. I know some think my attitude is foolish, and they just don't understand. I'll admit that sometimes those judgments hurt, but at the end of the day, God is whom I am led by; God is whom I am accountable to. The way I have grown in Him since our years through unthinkable hardship, brokenness, and defeat is immeasurable; and because of that, I can stand in what is disorderly and uncomfortable. For I walk by faith, not by sight—not because of what some think but because *I know* my God. I have seen His leading, unfolding, and faithfulness in so many areas, so I am expectant of those others who are a work in progress.

The Power of Light: December 1, 2014

I know it likely sounds absurd that a woman at the age of thirty-five was still afraid of the dark, but until recent times, that was my reality. If it was nighttime, I would joke and say I didn't want to do a myriad of things in case the boogeyman got me. Truth is, there was a real fear, and I was comfortable only if Brett was with me.

My mum has said that as a toddler I was a very confident, secure, happy child who was a good sleeper and fine with the whole bedtime routine. Then one day that changed, and while she tried to figure out whether there was an incident that brought this fear about, to this day she is still unsure. Suddenly I was terrified of the dark, and she needed to sit beside my bed until I went to sleep.

Events in years to come only fueled that fear. I still recall waking to various situations that were horrendous and gripped me with many emotions. Going to bed wasn't something I was a fan of, to say the least. Darkness of any kind wasn't my friend.

I remember that when we first got married, Brett discovered I wasn't a good sleeper. Even with him asleep beside me, I would wake and feel fearful as I lay awake for hours with the room pitch black. My overly creative and imaginative mind would only fuel my racing heart, much of it based on realities from my abuse or living in unsafe areas that had fights to be heard in the still of the night, and I feared were to begin again.

This year at the in-depth Bible study, I prepared to do the Bible story in the kid's program. It was the story from Matthew of the disciples in the boat and Jesus coming and calming the storm. One of the truths was that Jesus has power over all things. Fears were discussed at the end and that we could turn to Jesus to help us. The words I had prepared and taught stuck with me. As the weeks went by, I woke in the night, and for an instant that gripping fear came over me, but then I thought back to that lesson and realized I didn't need to be afraid. I opened my eyes, and the room wasn't pitch black and scary. Instead I felt peace and could sense light. How that thinking has altered things drastically.

I'd not thought of what I'm about to share for over fifteen years, but as I grappled with this fear and the truth taught, I've replayed a memory many times of late, but the power of prayer has comforted me. I was sixteen, and on the return from Australia, I went to stay with my sister and then two different friends, while my parents were still there. The one friend's mum dropped me off at another town to stay with the other friend for the week, but she told me that if anything made me fearful or uncomfortable, I should phone her, and she would pick me up early. She sensed that the father of this friend wasn't a nice man. I'd had uncomfortable experiences in the past I'd never spoken of, so it amazed me that she was sensitive to this reality.

That first night all was dark, and the household was fast asleep. I woke to hear footsteps. As they came closer, my heart raced, and I had a gripping fear that the intentions weren't good and that the uncomfortable moments were about to become more. I lay there with my body rigid and ready to fight. I prayed like never before. Then he appeared in the doorway right in front of my bed and stood for some moments. I continued to pray, keeping my body rigid, my eyes locking with a fierce sense of protection and power. I watched him soon return to where he'd come from. The next morning I phoned the mum and said I would like to be picked up that day, please, trusting my gut.

I have countless stories of how the power of Jesus and prayer altered events that could have ended so differently. God is indeed in control of all things. Now don't even try to get me to explain how that can be true given some of the awful realities in my life that have happened. I'm not someone who has all the answers. But what I do know is that John 10:10 is true of Satan, who tries to come like a thief in the night, seeking to kill and destroy. Even when he "succeeds," God can turn that success around, and I can attest to that fact on many fronts.

The power of light is tangible. How could knowing that power and reality alter your life? What fears grip you that you could allow that simple truth to turn around? I've got some more to work on now that the dark is taken care of, so how about we walk from fear into freedom on other points together?

The "If Only" Moments: December 4, 2014

I detest the lies Satan causes people to believe. He whispers into their lives, and that act is fueled and compounds until the person wrestles with many "if only" moments.

I had a childhood of abuse at the hands of those close to my family. It should never have happened, but it did. That abuse formed many struggles, most of which by God's work has been dealt with and restored, with other portions still a work in progress.

That abuse created a sense of shame, of self-hate and self-blame. I felt that I wasn't worthy of good, that anything bad that happened was my own doing—whether it be with abuse, friendships, family, infertility, or really anything in life. It made me highly aware of many things I shouldn't have had to be. What I believed was far from God's truth; I just didn't know it.

When I was seventeen and we were again living in a new city, I walked along the main road from school toward home. I passed through a busy bus stop and carried on along the many blocks toward my turnoff. As I neared that, I found it unusual that a guy was still following me and became scared. I thankfully had some fight in me since my childhood and decided to turn around and confront him while I was still on a main road. I asked him whether he was following me. It turns out he was. He had tried to catch up with me since the bus stop to get my number. He said he'd been taken with me and knew he'd kick himself if he didn't at least try. So ensued the pursuit, which received a dead end.

As I carried on home, I went through the thoughts of being thankful that he was odd but not threatening, beating myself up for getting in sticky situations too often and trying to figure out what to change and how to change myself to avoid these events. I wasn't anything special to look at by the world's standards or my own, so the problem had to be because I was too confident, happy, or smiley, as some people had said of me (which is a testament to God given my past and how much further it should have shaped me). So then ensued the years of trying to balance that desire to be invisible and the way God had created me to be.

Then just this year I had an incident at the gas station. A man came into the automated car wash as I sat in my car and was approaching me. I scared him off, thanks to God making me aware of his approach to the car and Brett having taught me what to do. As

I went home, I was thankful that all had ended okay, but as weeks passed, I wondered whether the problem was because my lip gloss was too attention grabbing, or maybe I had been smiling without realizing it as I went about my business, as seems to happen all too often. Over all these years, much thought has gone into how I dress and even how I act. But I couldn't help but again go down the "if only" and "what if" track as I began to wonder how to again change myself, as if the problem were on me.

How truly wrong it is that Satan whispers such strong lies to so many of us. I'm thankful God didn't let that wrong thinking take hold so I could continue growing in Him and finding the freedom to be myself to the fullest extent, as He'd created and intended all along.

Due to many experiences in my past, I've tried to find that balance between being who God naturally created me to be but reigning it in, because of many "if only" or "what if" moments. While it's right to grow, change, and develop, there is a real risk of diluting the person God created you to be to fit into the expected, to avoid hurts because of the world we live in, and so much more.

Having this year found freedom to be me in the fullness God created, I feel sad for myself that I missed out on that for so long because of Satan's lies and how society is. I wonder if you too are missing out on that freedom because of such things. Will you allow God to help you see the truths through the lies, to find your own solid footing in who He made you to be, to flourish and be free? Will you let go of the "if only" moments to enjoy your life now?

Those "if only" and "what if" moments don't just apply to what I've shared from my experiences. I know many who've had those moments over parenting, relationship decisions, and even business or financial choices. Pretty much everything we do or has been done to us in life can create those thoughts, big or small. So if you're in that cycle for whatever reason, how can you alter that to find peace, confidence, and freedom?

A Lesson in a Teapot: December 7, 2014

On Monday I had a lovely lady over for a cuppa and a chat. As I went about my morning of business paper work, exercise, and then preparation for her arrival, I decided to go all out, because I just love hosting and being able to do all the fun attention-to-detail things.

When Brett and I were in our early years of marriage, his grandmother wanted to give us this special tea set. David, her son; and Brett's father, who died when Brett was a toddler; had given it to her as a gift. She wanted us to have something that linked with him, as we were in this new chapter of life. Gail (my mother in law), in her usual wonderful ways, picked up on the fact that as a couple in our early twenties, newly married with a very modern home and palate, it wasn't something an overly organized minimalist wanted, while the sentiment was appreciated. Gail held onto it on our behalf for many years, without us knowing. Then when she knew the time was right, she passed it on to us.

Now the tea set didn't have a teapot with it, and in my particular ways I couldn't use it without one. So ensued the hunt for just the right teapot, which may not be an exact match but would work perfectly. It needed to be delicate, rounded, and just so. Numerous years passed, with us looking at many antique shops and home stores. Finally, last month I found it. This day I spied the pot and decided to go down a different track than what I'd thought for her visit and use it. Before I knew it, everything was set, and I took a photo to share with Brett, as I was so excited to finally be able to use it.

As this lady and I sat and chatted about all kinds of things, she asked where things were progressing on the home front, and then we discussed the baby front. I said that both were in the waiting stage at the hands of others, and while at times I found the experience frustrating, I was trusting in God and enjoying what I could. She remarked on the joy that was evident despite the waiting.

I joked about the fact that I wasn't good with patience, that even when I had been young, this trait had been evident. Yet there seemed to be a lot of waiting in my life. I shared that one day in Melbourne

(I think I was about four), I stood in the kitchen with my dad telling me about patience. He even sang me a song: "Have patience, have patience, don't be in such a hurry." I told him that God hadn't put patience in me when He made me, so I didn't see the need to learn it and went off on my merry way.

A bit later in the morning, when the conversation turned to the importance of the tea set, the search for the teapot. and my joy in this being the first time to use it, she remarked on my actually having a great deal of patience. She said most people wouldn't have held out to find just the right teapot; they would have found what would do and started using it. As she left, I pondered her words, as my response had been that anything good was worth the wait.

I'm someone who has a clear picture in my head on home things or even items for my wardrobe. I will look for something, but if I don't find it, I simply go without it until I find just the right thing. I don't ever want to settle for second best or have an attitude of "It will do." Sometimes finding what I want can take years for something most people would just give up on. But I'm rather particular and persistent, it would seem. As I thought over all this, I couldn't help but think about our own journey toward the finish line for our miracles. Yes, there is waiting and hardship in it, but my goodness, what a reward it will be when the day comes for what we've ached for, waited for, fought for, prayed for, hoped for, and even endured greatly for.

This can be a hard time of year for many for different reasons. With the putting up of our beautiful Christmas decorations, I have thought a great deal about those precious ladies I'm walking beside in their struggles right now. Out of a simple tea set has been a great deal of encouragement for me, and I hope it is for you too.

This doesn't discount the hardship in the waiting, but I hope it can be a ray of light in this moment. I hope that as you read the words of how much patience and effort I take with a teapot to use a special tea set, you will reflect on how much more patience and effort God takes with you.

God is growing us all to know Him, to have characters that radiate what is Christ like. God sees the big picture. He knows full well what is ahead and what is needed for it to unfold. He doesn't want to settle for second best for us just because our patience or trust isn't quite up to scratch in that moment.

I like to picture God sitting there with a beaming smile, glorious light surrounding Him, and His eyes the picture of depth and exuding love. While He sees me having a little "tanty" over my reality at times, He whispers, "My dear one, I have better ahead if you will just wait and keep trusting." In the times of tears and heartache, He gently places His hand on my shoulder, draws me in, wipes my tears, and says, "It saddens me too that you feel the weight, but will you remember to place your burdens with Me, to trust in Me, to walk with Me and know I have you even in this? The day is coming, my precious daughter, when all this will be behind you and you will be pleased that I didn't shortchange you simply to satisfy the now."

The best things in life are worth waiting for, searching for, and fighting for. I've already seen evidence of that fact in my ten-plus years of being "a mum in waiting." Will you too look beyond the reality to see the evidence and worth in this? Will you give your burdens to God and trust Him to be all you need in the waiting? I hope so, because I've been in that state of brokenness and anger, and I know all too well what it can rob you of, just as I now know how God can swoop in to restore, grow, and provide. What will be your choice and outcome in the waiting, in the season of hardship?

What a difference a few days can make. Last week I drafted the above blog and felt so thankful for the lesson and felt a boost of hope in the waiting. However, I waited on publishing it because I didn't want to bombard you.

Come Friday I had one of those days that sneaks up on you and knocks you off your feet. I felt such sadness, such loneliness, because my December was so very different from that of my friends and family. By the time Brett came home from work, the tears flowed, and the words tumbled out. I looked at him and asked whether this would finally be the last December like this. How could this be our eleventh December of this ache, this reality? While I love my life, while God helps me hugely on this journey, and while I have the best husband in the world, who makes such a difference, they don't stop those days that come out of nowhere so you feel the reality acutely. You and others who walk this road get it.

I felt like a hypocrite having this blog in drafts, because days later I felt so different. Then this morning I woke, and my devotional had the gist of "God acts for those who wait on Him." So while I have days that knock me off my feet, I have a God who knows just the words I need. I have a husband who will hold me, listen, and brighten my dark days. So here I am, posting but adding to the bottom to show I get it, but I hope this can encourage both you and me in those days that knock us off our feet. God has us in *all* things.

'Tis the Season of Survival for Some: December 10, 2014

Ever since I was a little girl and watched an American lady decorate her home with such careful detail and over-the-top joy, and open it up for celebrations, I came to love Christmas in a different way. I remember our first year of married life. I told Brett that I wanted to take a leaf out of her book, and so ensued our own traditions and over-the-top ways.

But as the years passed and more notches were added to our belt of infertility, a sadness crept into the mix of the joy and traditions. While the true meaning of Christmas and the impact on my faith remained, the other portions waned. I admit that 2010 to 2012 are a bit of a blur to me, when it comes to December and Christmas Day. I know that those times held losses beyond comprehension, quality of life affected by fertility medication, and an ache so enormous it doesn't bear thinking of.

One of our traditions that started on our first Christmas was a DVD in the stocking to watch that night once it was just us again. We know that tradition missed a few years but is back on for this one, as was putting up the decorations for the first of the month. The constant joy and excitement of last year aren't there; though they aren't the blur of past ones, there are no losses as such and certainly no debilitating medications to affect things. But life is a mixed bag all the same. There is partial joy and excitement but also a real ache, sadness, and dread.

As has been the way for the past few years, we don't do stockings and presents under the tree for each other, because doing so is just too hard. We don't do the all-out Christmas breakfast because it just feels hollow. Instead we hold each other as tears roll down my cheeks at the lack when we first wake. We eat a normal breakfast and distract ourselves with TV, then get ready and head to family events. When our home has miracles, we will again do those traditions, and the emotions will no longer be mixed.

I share this reality to show that I do get that this is the season of survival for many and that even when there is hope in God and assurances for tomorrow, this is a time when children are the focus in many households, and they only highlight the emptiness in our homes. While December is the busiest time of year for most, it's my quietest time of year. That fact has been acutely apparent this year, which is why I think Christmas is such a mixed bag for me and why I've hit a big bump in the road.

We've all read the helpful tips out there from fertility clinics and support groups. You know the drill of making your needs as priority, pulling back from hard family events, doing social activities with friends who don't have children, being honest about what you need to get through, and so forth. But that can be a little harder for those who love family and would hate to miss out on portions of it, who don't really have friends without kids and whose people are all super busy with this time of year, meaning that what we need can't really happen.

I can't say my tips are sure proof, as my own struggle is proof that they're not. But these are some issues I had time to mull over when I was in the car yesterday for many hours while on a trip:

- Don't pull back from family activities but maybe just make them a bit more consolidated and concise.
- Allow yourself time out from your own traditions and ways if they only add to the struggle and find ways that work for you as a couple.
- Let yourself off the hook and feel and process all that is needed. The reality of your lack is actually more significant than most realize. So give yourself a break.
- Accept that this is a time of year when others will become absorbed with their busyness and not take into consideration that you are struggling and that it's a time when you need support. Show them grace during that time and remember that this road has likely already shown you who your real people are. Those people deserve your allowances and understanding.
- Understand that some may take your concerns into consideration but find it awkward to know whether it's best to broach them or leave them be. Again grace, allowances, and understanding are required. And yes, I get that sometimes being the one to show understanding doesn't feel fair, and you want it to be about you for just one moment! But do extend grace anyway.
- If you find you have time on your hands, as I do, then find projects to keep you occupied to avoid wallowing. (I for one have done gardening, paper work, and errands for others to ease their load. I have watched a crazy amount of Christmas movies, researched, and made purchases to try out nail art— just to name a few.)
- Press into God in a variety of ways. I know some may groan, but this really makes a difference. Do some in depth study of the bible. I've listened to worship music as I do housework, watched YouTube sermons while baking, read books, and even sat on the floor and let it all out to God. He has all the time in the world for you.

– Remember, you aren't the only one struggling with this time and the realities of infertility. While you may feel alone with your problem, I find it helpful to know that others do understand. I also find it helpful to remember that December isn't just hard for me. It's also difficult for those who've lost a loved one through death or divorce, are dealing with terminal illness, or are single (not by choice) and struggling, as are those dealing with family hurts or feuds, and the list goes on. As a result, I try to be outward focused and do big or small things for others in their time of hardship, which I admit isn't always easy.

Know that in this time of survival, I get it, I care, and if needed I am here.

Yet Will I Trust: December 13, 2014

As the end of another year approaches, one usually looks back and reflects. On the whole as I do so, I see how faithful my God is. There have been milestones reached that I thought would never need to be endured, but by His grace there was joy that passes all understanding. There were more friendships altered, more hard decisions to be made, and yet more waiting at God's feet. But what stands out to me are the moments when God grew me, drew me closer, carried me, freed me, and healed me. The works that are within and unseen are what this year brought as the highlights, truly my foundation year, my gift from God beyond measure.

I have always been a dreamer, someone who would expect the best but then, should that not unfold, would accept the realities but then dream once more. This December was no different. I had thought how wonderful it would be during this month to see God's timing for our miracles. Others clearly longed for the same with their messages of hope that this would be like no other.

This week started with my grappling with emotions as I hit a bump in the road. I sat on the floor, which seems to be where I do all my serious business with God. My legs folded, my body crumpled down onto the carpet, and with the tears flowing, I expressed where I was and what I longed for. I also said that with this year I had seen to a greater extent that His ways are so much higher and better than mine, and I entrusted my hopes and dreams into His hands for His timing and unfolding.

Later on that week, I found that the bookstore had finally gotten the stock, and I could pick up *Never Give Up!* by Joyce Meyer. As it sat there, looking at me, I wanted so much to be able to read it through different times with different eyes. But before I could even read a word, I found myself back to day one, with yet another disappointment, yet another year closing without the longed-for miracles. I had a new year to begin in the same season I had been in for so very long.

In fact, I'd read a blog that Fertility NZ had shared, and the lady had dealt with twenty-one cycles of disappointment. Out of curiosity I added up what our number of circles were, and being over one-hundred-and-twenty, I saw just why this felt like a marathon of a lifetime. *Really, God, couldn't this end now?* Why did there need to be another one added to the notch? As I lay in bed, awake in the small hours of the morning, speaking to God about things, He told me, *With Me you can get through all days, and I promise You my timing is perfect, and I do have You in this.*

Okay, God, yet will I trust You.

While I'm not one to give up hope, to let go of dreams, I felt like it was just too hard to start a new year full of hope and expectation for that to be the year. How many years could I naïvely start that way? How many more cycles could I pray for and invest in, hoping it to be the one? Maybe I could just have a holiday as such and let someone else carry the torch in the race. But with God's whispers to me in the night, and with reading the first few pages of the book yesterday evening, I know that when we don't give up, beautiful things can happen with God.

I will trust my God as I continue to dream, hope, expect, and invest, ... all the while knowing that He has got me in this, that His timing is perfect, and that with Him I can indeed get through all days.

Finding Life and Beauty amid It All: December 20, 2014

These weeks have been a mixed bag for me. There has been sadness at the reality of another year closing without my longed-for miracles while wondering what next year holds and enduring all that comes with being in a very different season from my family and friends, including the loneliness this situation brings. But there have also been wonderful reminders as I've met with some extraordinary and resilient women through the book. Their questions have reminded me of just what hope I do have in God, what goodness is in my life, what truths I have gleaned through the years on this road. I also recall who I am now and how far I have come.

This morning I had an encounter with a dear lady over the screen of my laptop. I was again reminded of some wonderful truths. I couldn't help but gaze at the beautiful roses growing in our planter box and think about the significance. You see, buried in that planter box are many of our lost embryos; with them are buried the possible miracles, some hopes and dreams. There is much sadness and grief mixed in with it all. Below the surface of the soil lies brokenness, defeat, and many unpleasant emotions, unspoken words, and unshared realities; above the soil is a plant that has been resilient in this recent weather bomb we have had. The rose bush is covered with so many beautiful flowers and buds that life and beauty ooze from them.

I can't help but reflect on how that rose bush and what lays beneath is symbolic of the road that has been walked, the lessons learned, and the realities for us. There are indeed heartbreaking and unthinkable parts of our history; there are portions that are unseen, but they don't negate their existence or how they shape who we are. Nor do the parts that aren't so glossy and nice define who we are, what our lives are, or what the future holds. Out of brokenness and darkness can grow extraordinary platforms for strength, resilience, appreciation for life, blessings, balance, and priorities—aspects those who haven't had that experience can't glean to the same extent. As I reflect on the words of a lady and this Christmas and what it encompasses, I can't help but take my pondering a step further.

Those who are Christians believe in a God who loved us so much that He sent His one and only Son to be born into humanity in the most miraculous way. He sent His Son to walk on this earth, where there were trials and joys, and to then be given the greatest task of sacrificing His life and enduring much so we could gain life to its fullest for eternity. We know the reality of the most rare and defining gift.

We know from the Bible that we're not immune to difficulties, but in them we have a God we can lean on. He will carry us, grow us in them, and unfold beauty from ashes. We know that buds will come, and they will then blossom. So while the current road for you and I may not be all we want, and while the world may be able to look at only what is and not what is beneath, we know the costs that have been paid. We know what has been endured to shape who we are, just like we know what can come from such experiences, what life and beauty are amid it all. Jesus is a prime example of what overwhelmingly good gifts and life can come from the greatest sacrifice and endurance. Your sacrifice and mine are but a dot in the ocean of His, but they still hold significance on both fronts if we let them. Don't let Satan rob you of what can come or what can be gained. Instead let God pour out, unfold, and do all He is waiting and longing to do, for He alone can bring forth change, healing, growth, and all that has worth. We just need to be willing, and He will do the rest.

Just like this rose bush for me, there are unpleasant histories buried beneath, but there is growth through them. While I may have shared about my darkest days with some this month, and while I may have remembered things I had forgotten in doing so, I know I've moved on from them. Yes, I still may have struggles and aches, and the darkness will always be in my history. But there is also the work at the hand of my ever-faithful God, where He has blossomed me and grown me, defining me in His beauty and grace. Through them He is unfolding a purpose, and I can know that what is ahead is more growth, adventure, and the fruition of old dreams and new dreams, of hope realized, and of a walk with Him taken to greater and deeper levels through it all. So will you too see the beauty in the ashes? Will you allow Him to blossom you and choose life so it is all it can be?

You have the power to choose death or life. What will it be for you?

The Hope in Christmas: December 25, 2014

"Behold, I bring you good tidings of great joy, which shall be for all people. For unto you is born this day ... a Savior, which is Jesus Christ the Lord." based on Luke 2:10-11

Today may be tinged with sadness for you because of many reasons—you may be aching for your own long-awaited miracle. You may have lost a loved one, and perhaps the pain is still raw. You may be estranged from family at such a time. Whatever the reason, I know full well it can be extenuated on this day when family is such a focal point.

I feel for you in this time of longing and pain, when emotions are heightened. Trust me, I get it all too well. But may I encourage you that today we celebrate the birth of Jesus, the only One who is fully God and fully man, the only One who paid the ultimate price for us to have the ultimate gift.

Today marks the beginning of the greatest hope of all, His birth all those years ago and what we celebrate on this day. We believe in Him, accept Him as Lord, know Him, and are transformed by His power. We have certainty of eternity and security of a personal and constant Savior and Friend. All these blessings and more are what today can represent. That is a hope that is immeasurable. That is a hope that is life changing and extravagant.

So while we may wipe tears, may we also turn our eyes to a Savior and Friend who knows where we've been, where we are, and where we are going—and in it all He is with us. My prayer for you and me is that in the midst of the celebrations, when they may be tinged with sorrow, that we will know a hope and joy that are indescribable, those that can bring what truly matters.

On that note, dear one, I think of you, I pray for you on this day, and I wish you a Merry Christmas. I trust that you will find the true hope that today holds for you and that in that you will find a peace that surpasses all understanding.

A New Year Dawns: January 6, 2015

It is no secret that December was a very hard month for me. The difficulty took me by surprise, which made it all the harder. I wasn't looking forward to Christmas Day at all and was even loathing the start of a new year. But days before, God started putting details into place to turn things around for me.

My dear friend and her daughter came to spend the day with me on the Friday before Christmas. We made Christmas tree shortbread cookies and decorated them, we watched *Home Alone*, and I even purchased music on iTunes so we could listen to Christmas music while we went about the day's activities.

At the end, her daughter raced around each room, looking at my decorations. When they left, I saw she had altered the nativity set in the most beautiful way. Instead of the pieces being outwardly focused, to make them look pretty, she had made them inwardly focused to be all about the baby. That fact sat with me as I reflected on how Christmas is the day our Savior was born, the One worthy of praise and adoration, of focus and reflection. That is what it is truly about.

When Christmas morning came, I woke with Christmas carols that adore Him on my lips. The tears weren't there, as I could feel the prayers of those near and dear, and I know my Lord tilted my chin from being down about my reality to being lifted and focused on Him.

When Brett woke, we had a hug and wished each other a Merry Christmas, but there weren't the usual ache and outpouring of tears.

Instead we sat by the tree, which had a gift from me to us of hope: three little duckies. (Those who've read *A Mum in Waiting* will know the significance and Brett's tattoo, so how fitting this was as we went into the eleventh year on this road.)

Then my dear friend had placed a very thoughtful gift under the tree days earlier. It had the most beautiful letter with words of understanding, hope, and encouragement. Then certain words were colored and matched a gift within the Santa sack. At the bottom there was the idea of passing on the Christmas kindness to someone in my shoes next year, and I can't wait for God to lead me to who the person will be so I can go about doing that.

After the gift time, we sat outside in the sun and chatted, even putting in effort for a special breakfast. At no point were there tears or the need to watch TV and escape the ache and dull the senses. Then the time with the two sides of family was so fun, so special, and it was just the icing on the cake to a wonderful day. I could see God's grace and hand in it all.

Over the years there have been many well-wishes as a New Year dawns, certainties that this would be the year for our miracles. And while I love that people want this gift for us so much, I no longer am as naïve and know that our hopes, dreams, and prayers don't always come to fruition in the longed-for time.

As this New Year has dawned, it's been no different with the well-wishes than in previous years. But there have also been more sincere words given, where we could see God at play. And there has been a common thread of it being the dawn of new beginnings, with joy after sorrow, it being a year of jubilee. God's plans and purposes come to fruition after the purposed years of hard slogs, even images of butterflies (you may remember their significance from the post about new beginnings after the ten year anniversary was reached), and so much more. Naturally I want to take those words on board and conclude that they are God's assurance that 2015 will be the year for our miracles. While there is expectation and longing for this fact to be so, I know better after many years around this block and many incredible words given.

When God gives a word in various forms and through various people, it does hold weight; don't get me wrong here. But I've also seen many years start with people full of expectations for one goal coming to fruition and instead see it close with a different one unfolding. So I go into this year with my eyes wide open, my heart full of hope, my prayers confident with expectation, my faith strengthened by my God, and an assurance that this year will indeed be one of new beginnings, joy, and growth taking flight in all He unfolds. I just don't know what that means or how it looks.

As this New Year dawns, I'm so incredibly excited. I'm so looking forward to starting again at the in-depth Bible study I go to in February and studying the life of Moses. I know that through it God will encourage me, grow me, refine me, and unfold all He has purposed for me to learn to be the person He has for me to be. I know I will take flight with Him and, experience new depths, greater joy, and new beginnings.

I am also very excited about this year being one filled with fun moments and special people. I'm expectant for many highlights in the year because of it. It is a year when my dear auntie and her wonderful husband visit in February. Then in April some special friends have asked us to join them on holiday, which will be incredible. Come June our much-loved old youth pastors will come to stay as a family, and my heart could just burst over this visit. Then in July the joy doesn't stop because my parents will move back to New Zealand after many years being away, and I even get to meet our "adopted brother" on their return. And of course there will be many special moments with all those regulars in my life whom I adore and have such great times with.

There are so many things to look forward to in this year on many fronts. I am expectant for our miracles but know that even if this too isn't the year God has good in store for us, I can trust Him and rejoice in all He unfolds.

So how about you? With this New Year dawning, is the unknown crushing your soul and causing you to flounder in your walk with God? Do you long for control so badly that you will allow yourself to miss all the guaranteed gems? I've been there, my friend. I do get it, but I just hope that you won't allow too many years to be wasted in that land, in the wilderness. Do allow yourself those moments to grieve, process, and navigate, as we all need to when life's curve balls drag on. Just don't remain there. Get up again because each day dawns with beauty, with unexpected goodness, if we will just look up to see it.

My Roller Coaster Sabbatical: January 29, 2015

Yesterday wasn't at all the day I had planned; in fact, it was very far from it. I had an incident occur, where I bled and I was on the phone with the doctors; and as I awaited the call back, I told God that no matter what unfolded, I knew I could trust Him. No matter what, I was confident that He had our best at heart and that the bad would never negate the good that had been promised.

Then the phone rang, and I dashed to the doctors for an appointment and blood work. My history was discussed, understanding looks were given, tears were wiped, and I left, knowing that a day would tick by before there was a possible known. I was told that I could face a miscarriage, and if that wasn't the case, then something else was going on, and further tests would be done to get to the bottom of my incident.

During the drive home, the tears flowed. I hadn't known there was a possible baby to hope for, to dream of, or to fall in love with. If this was a miscarriage, that broke my heart more than the other disappointments. If this wasn't that, then I had no idea what it could be, but the doctor's reaction didn't leave me feeling like it was an overly easy or good thing. I was frustrated that we may have extras added to our plates when we were enjoying a blissful life of trusting and waiting, which was far easier than roller coasters, blood work, and appointments.

When reaching home, I updated the few near and dears with the news and asked them to pray for us in the waiting as things unfolded. I voiced my heartache over feeling like I was on the roller coaster of waiting and wondering, heartache and complications. Didn't the world know I was on sabbatical from that? Come on, give a girl a break.

The tears subsided. I got on with doing my nails so I was all ready for our twelve-year anniversary celebrations coming up, and then God began to work within me. Yes, this situation was far from ideal. But the truth remained that He was my anchor, that I would never be forsaken, that in all things I could trust Him, and so much more. We had a wonderful evening together, and then I had a great sleep as I rested in God's assurances with the love of my life beside me.

This morning, as I read my timely devotional and then went out and watered my roses and spent time with God, the thought dawned on me. While our circumstances that may dictate the sabbatical from the roller coaster are over, this doesn't actually mean we need to oblige. A choice can be made. When we are anchored in God and when His truths are real to us and we can bring it all to Him, we can stay on the platform and not get on that loathed ride that was too familiar in years gone by.

So today I refuse to rejoin the ride. I instead choose to stay grounded with my God, knowing that I can enjoy today as I await the news from the doctors and whatever unfolds from here. For today the sun shines; the blessings and goodness that had me smiling when I woke yesterday are still here. How about you? Will you be on the platform or the ride?

And So a New Season Begins: March 11, 2015

How fitting, as March brings a new season, that I too start a new season of life. It's not one I expected; it's not the one I longed to announce, but it is a new one all the same, one that has been marinating. I approach it with a great deal of excitement, a deep sense of trust in my God, and incredible anticipation—and if I'm honest, a bit of fear too.

As you likely know, God told me in my teen years that He had a call on my life, and I tried to run from it, a flight that was successful for some time. However, in mid-2013 He captured my heart in such a way that I couldn't be disobedient when He called me to be a kid's leader for the Bible study I go to weekly. He told me it was the first of many stepping-stones to what He had for me. He intended to grow me in each for what He truly had ordained. I tried excuses, reminded Him of my flaws, told Him it seemed cruel given our lack, and suggested other people I thought were better suited for the job; but in the end, I said yes.

I reflect on that time as it comes to an end eighteen months later and know that in that time God has worked significantly. My life has been turned upside down in a great way. That season has been a time of Him restoring me on every single front. He has reignited my love for Him and my heart for serving; He has reestablished my desire to walk the path He has for me and to walk out my purpose as He unfolds it, whatever it looks like. It has been a time when I've felt unconditional love, absolute forgiveness, and complete freedom with my ever-faithful God on a whole new level. Also, it was a time where I got to love other people's kid's and have the ache for my own dulled somewhat. Psalm 23:3 is so fitting. "He refreshes and restores my life. He leads me along the right path for His name sake."

He has been preparing me for this season's ending and a new one starting. In September last year, God told me serving in kid's wasn't forever. However, in my human mind I decided I had another five years of serving in kid's. Surely with my tendencies I would be a long time at each stepping-stone and be ancient when I reached the call

He had intended all along and was growing me toward. In November last year, He told me 2015 held new seasons, and one was to invest in women. I once again decided that meant that on the side I would help women through the book and be a little more purposeful. I would have the courage to speak to their lives in the way God led me to. Then this year, when I prayed about the year ahead, He gave me three verses to hold onto for what He had ahead.

"Sometime later God tested Abraham. He said to him, Abraham, Here I am, he replied" (Gen. 22:1). *Okay, God, I can get on board with that. You want me to be available and obedient.*

"Have I not commanded you? Be strong and courageous. Do not be terrified; do not be discouraged, for the Lord your God will be with you wherever you go" (Josh. 1:9). *Oh dear, please don't give me that one. That is what You used with the book launch, but as it sat with me, I was thankful for the reminder, though I was a little terrified as to what that could be ahead.*

"For I know the plans I have for you, declares the Lord, plans to prosper you and not harm you, plans to give you a hope and a future" (Jer. 29:11). *Well, of course, God. I know that one, but why are You reminding me of that?*

A month passed, and Fertility NZ approached me and asked me to do some things for them that would take up a lot of my time. As I sat on the matter and sought God, I felt that I should turn the opportunity down; though some aspects of the role fit with what God seemed to be calling me to in terms of being on a stage, it wasn't it. He needed my time to be available to invest in a special group of women in the way He'd ordained. *Okay, God, I get it. I'll say no, wait, and while doing so pray for these unknown women. But please let me keep doing kids, regardless of what You unfold.*

Then a call came a week later, and God was moving me from one season to another. He indeed had me give up the kids and invest in a group of women. So this wasn't at all what I'd imagined. When I hung up the phone, I didn't even get a moment to tell God my excuses, my buts, and my ifs. Instead He spoke, and all I could do was internally nod.

Am I not the director of your path?

Did I not warn you this was coming … not to get too comfortable with kids, that it wasn't forever?

Did I not warn you that change was coming and even tell you that you were to invest in women, that you could trust Me in all that?

And didn't I tell you this was the first stepping-stone and that the time would come to move on?

You are to say yes and leave the rest to Me. I am your God. You can trust Me. Have I not proved that so many times?

Then just as I was about to get a "but" out, God interrupted and said, *Do you not think that I have taken that into account? I will sort out the ache.* (This is where my mind went into dreamland, and I decided I'd be pregnant that cycle and have twins in December.) *Before you go racing ahead*—I'd quickly snapped out and was listening again—*the details are My business.*

There went the wishful thinking of getting pregnant that cycle and having my own babies to take away the ache. Or maybe it didn't, but the point was to *trust*! God had me in all things. And how timely to be studying the life of Moses and to mull over the truths that God helps those He calls, that our imagination doesn't limit His works. Oh, what a God I get to know, walk with, and serve.

I'd love to say that I *graciously* responded with a yes, but while there was a yes, there were tears, a "tanty," a pity party, and plenty of self-doubt. Then after a day came anticipation and excitement as I reflected on just how big my God is and how extravagantly and faithfully He loves me, provides for me, and leads me. I can know full well that I don't actually need to fear all the lies Satan has whispered, because my God has got me in all things. Is it not far better to walk His path than my own? Yes, it is. When will I grasp it in its fullness and avoid this silliness?

So here's to a new season …

How about you? Is God calling you into a new season? Will you follow Him? Or will you miss out on the perfection and abundance He has in store?

Reality Check: April 15, 2015

Today as I sit here and look out the window, the weather is gloomy, and the temperature cold. Oh, how nice it would be to be overseas on holiday again. It's not always easy getting back into normal life, as much as I do actually love it. And a change in season can actually create the blues, as much as I am excited about being able to layer and change from the summer wardrobe I got sick of.

As I sat processing, I reflected on a number of things.

On our holiday with friends, their adorable nine-year-old girl made me smile on so many occasions. I loved hanging out in the pool and beach with her, going on the slide countless times, and just having a kid around. She excuses my being a big kid at heart. Then I went home to a wonderful weekend with family, and I know it sounds crazy, but even the tears and tantrums that were had made my heart swell with longing for one day. I don't want to pump my head with air, but I feel like I'm a natural at it. However, that wave of doubt came in when talking with a friend who was also in a similar space with me, and I wondered whether my being on this journey for over ten and a half years now with Brett meant we were too deeply in the couple life to be able to successfully move to family life when that time came. What if I couldn't cope when it was 24-7 entertaining, caring for babies, comforting them, playing referee, and doing so much more? What if I would fail these longed-for miracles. Even those doubts didn't stop me from wishing God would hasten His pace with what had been promised so many times. I feel like I'm becoming the boy who cried wolf; with all this time passing, it seems that fewer people expect the outcome I am. It's feeling like a rather lonely space to wait in.

Yesterday I reached my limit with some of the "dramas" we'd come home to. I didn't feel like the loving, compassionate, godly person who could walk in the shoes God had for me. I didn't see that the call God had for me in the now and in the future was sustainable for someone who was feeling flat and tired. It all just seemed too hard; the growing and giving were simply unsustainable in the now, let alone for the long term.

Last night, as I tossed and turned, wrestling over other people and feeling like it wasn't fair that much was expected of me when "they" could coast along, I had a dream. It wasn't an overly pleasant one, but something in it stuck with me. Sometimes it can be tiring to be you, to do for others and follow the path God has for you. It can even be isolating and lonely at times. But if you could just turn your eyes to see the deep reward, the pure joy that being you brings, and the many other countless benefits, the grumbles would soon disappear. If God said, *Okay, if you are just going to grumble about this privilege, then I can take it away and leave you as you were*, the very thought would have me in a panic. We can't pick and choose; life is the whole package or nothing at all. I know what I'd go with every time, even when having the blues.

The past week has had moments of frustration and the desire to be selfish, as it seems to be one thing after another. But I know that God has spent much time grooming my character, and although it would feel like a holiday to pick up old habits, it would be a great disservice to myself. So I push aside the urge to make it all about me, to feel hard done by with the harsh words and judgments of others, to shrink from the hard parts of this road God has me on. It's time to have a reality check. In the now what I need is my God, and He will help me to have the right attitude, turn things around once again, and make this a season of spreading joy, thriving, giving, and doing so much more.

How about you? Are you in a season that is hard, long, and lonely? Have you momentarily found yourself in a slump in the road too? Will you turn to God and allow Him to scoop you up and dust off the negativity you or others have brought into your space? Then will you allow God to focus your eyes on the rainbows, on the delights the now has? In so doing, you will be able to soar in this very moment and see God turn it into all it can be. Will you join me in once again letting God be God and stand back in wonder at the work of His hands once more?

What Mother's Day Holds: May 5, 2015

This Sunday is looming quickly, and it's one with a difference, because once again it's Mother's Day. The mention of that day can stir up many different emotions for people.

I know for some women I walk alongside, this day will have a particular sting to it since they are in the process of grieving a loss or fearful of impending treatments. It's such a hard road to navigate as you try to balance hope and self-protection, along with all the other emotions the day brings.

Then there are the women I've walked alongside who've now graduated and will be overcome with joy, as they are finally able to feel their precious one within kick or better yet to hold that baby in their arms. They've allowed the glee of the long-awaited miracle to diminish what has been for what is now.

This can feel like a slap in the face for those of us who are still longing, waiting, and wondering, but there are still those other sets of women who *are* mothers, but the day doesn't mean much to them. They are busy with the chaos of life. They are tired and struggle with realities we can't empathize with very easily.

And the list goes on ... For women who have estranged grown-up children, this day will cut to the core. The day will be tough for women who are single and wish to be in even our situation. Thankfully there is another set of women whom this day will have great meaning for; they are mothers, and they feel thankful and enjoy the season of life they are in.

Wherever you sit in this spectrum, if the day holds a pang and is a struggle, I pray that you too will be able to cling to God's sufficient grace. May we be able to reflect on 2 Timothy 1:12. "I know whom I have believed, and am convinced that *He will guard what I have entrusted to Him for that day*" (emphasis added). This verse paints a beautiful picture for me; there is much I entrust to my God. I can be assured that He will guard my emotions. He will guard the outpouring of sustaining grace and strength He's provided. He will guard the hopes, plans, dreams, and promises He has written on my heart. He will guard the timing of all that will unfold and bring it to completion in His perfect timing and way.

So here are my questions to you: Will you also entrust God to guard you and your emotions, hopes, life, and all? And if you aren't there yet, will you ask Him for help to get there?

My friends, wherever you find yourself this Sunday, I want you to know that you are not forgotten, that your reality is seen and does matter, that you aren't alone in this. And dare I even ask that you look beyond yourself and show care and grace to those around you, even if they are in another part of the spectrum than you are?

Deeper Obedience, Surrender, and Trust: May 15, 2015

This year in the weekly Bible study I go to, we are studying the life of Moses. As has been proved in the four years of studying God's Word in such an in-depth and layered way (Isaiah in 2011, Acts in 2012, Genesis in 2013, and Matthew in 2014), it is transforming and brings richness to knowing God. I approached this year with great excitement and expectation. It's only May and hasn't disappointed. In fact, I'd say this year has brought a greater level of richness and growth at the hands of my ever-faithful God.

Today I reflect back on 2011, when I nervously inquired about the in-depth Bible study and went along to the first Friday. My old youth pastor's wife had told me about it when we were driving to the Grand Canyon with their family for Brett's thirtieth birthday. I had shared with Angela that I was on debilitating fertility medication, that our first IVF was looming, and that the previous year had seen me hit rock bottom after many losses, much heartache, and some questioning of all I believed. I knew that if I was to come out on the other side of the year, I needed to sink my teeth into God's Word in a way that could anchor me, allow me to find God in a real way again, and put the broken pieces back together. Faith was the only way I knew how.

Sure, I'd been brought up in a Christian home. I'd even been involved in leadership of sorts and had peaks with God. There were indeed those key moments when I seemed to stand out from the crowd and wasn't afraid to stand up for my God, and I did have an active and real relationship with Him. People looked on and thought I had it all together, that I had a deep faith. Maybe I did to some extent, but I knew what was going on inside and understood that in all reality I was very undernourished when it came to knowing God's Word and having a good biblical knowledge. I needed to change that, and I knew that was the key to surviving all that was still to come.

When I think back to that broken girl, who was so far from God, disillusioned, and lost, I am floored at how far God has brought me in the past four years. He has indeed done a work beyond belief. His presence and His Word have certainly seen me forever changed. And this year He is taking me to new levels, where deeper obedience, surrender, and trust are required. Through the life of Moses, He has been teaching, growing, stretching, and equipping me for this coming season.

This past month has brought a number of key happenings.

I started my role as group leader with the women at the weekly Bible study and have already seen God's faithfulness as I learn and invest into what He has for me. The ladies are lovely and blessing me more than I am them. I'm gleaning new skills and just loving it.

I made the call to delete my personal Facebook page to free myself from the negativity on there and from the way it damages relationships in subtle ways and sucks valuable time. Yes, I'd been concerned about losing touch with some people and missing out. But there is joy in not being sucked into that world on a whole, and there is less emotional clutter. That's not to mention that there's now time to pray for someone in the grocery line instead of "checking in"; there's time to pick up a book and glean from God when dinner is prepped and I'm waiting on Brett's return home. Rearranging the apps on my phone has allowed me to have the audible NIV up first, so I click on that and get to soak in more of God's Word many moments in the week too. It's wonderful!

The elusive call from the fertility clinic finally came, and I must admit that I was shocked, as I'd not expected it after all this time. They said we had fallen through the cracks, and they offered the next round of IVF to us if we wanted. For a split second, my heart raced; my head was in a whirlwind. Was God now opening the door? Was this Satan distracting me, as IVF had seemed like a clear no before? What were we to do? With much prayer and discussion, God made the decision clear to me, and Brett was supportive. The clinic phoned, and the treatment was declined. I was nervous because of what people may say but at peace with the decision. I knew I needed to put action to my faith, that I needed to be obedient, surrender, and trust God to a deeper level. I was accountable to God and needed to disregard the whispers of Satan and the vocal words of some. This wasn't us closing the door on our road to parenthood; this wasn't us letting go of the promise for our miracles. This was simply planting feet on God's path in surrender and expectation. We were ending one chapter and beginning another.

Days later I once again had a mid cycle bleed and was on the phone to the doctor. There is no explanation as to why this suddenly happened, but I had peace about it. I wasn't going to get myself wound up, scream for answers, or demand anything. My God had proved Himself faithful on many occasions. I knew He had me. I wouldn't be rocked, for my anchor was secure.

I've realized that there is a cost to what lies ahead. I realize that to whom much is given, much is expected. Such calls and promises don't come on a silver platter. Steps are involved; action is required. Some steps are easy, and others are not. I can see that now is the time for me to implement what I feel God is calling me to do to ready myself for what He is unfolding. I can't expect change without action.

I don't know when or how God will unfold the call He has on my life in the bigger sense or what steps are in between now and then. I don't know when or how our miracles will come to be, but I believe to the very core of my being that each miracle will happen. And right now I'm in a season of readiness, allowing God to lay the foundations and stepping into a deeper level of obedience, surrender, and trust. While I'm in that space, I feel so overwhelmingly blessed that God brought along the right man to walk this road with me. He isn't timid or weak; he has guts, strength, and character. I feel his support, validation, and love with each step that unfolds. This true and rare gift makes my heart soar and a smile break across my face so many times of every single day.

So what about you? Where could God be calling you to pursue Him and His ways? What will your response be?

Give Yourself Permission: May 26, 2015

No matter what walk of life we go through, patches of being weighed down with a to-do list just feel a bit much to juggle. Whether you are a working woman, a stay-at-home mum, or someone running a business, serving in ministry, or doing a mix of all those things, we all have those weeks.

The other week I'd been wearing my many hats, and with the weekend that lay ahead, I had to take plates to two functions. I'd set aside some of Friday afternoon to do a triple batch of cookies. Usually I love baking, cooking, presenting things nicely, and going above and beyond. I enjoy this activity and don't feel burdened by it. But this particular week, I just had so much going on that I wasn't sure how to fit it in with some unexpected things that came up for that allotted time.

I gave myself permission; instead of feeling the pressure to find that extra time and run myself ragged, I popped down to the supermarket and purchased packet biscuits and drinks instead. It seemed like the cheats way and didn't go with my usual ways. For a split second, I wondered what others would think. Then it dawned on me that I don't take note of what others do, and they likely don't take note of what I do. Sure, there are times when people make comments, but I don't need to live up to those expectations; after all, the only reason I did "Tal way" was because I loved it. If I can't or wouldn't love it, then maybe I need to give myself permission not to in those moments. After all, what I do isn't about them; it's about me. We shouldn't create this false pressure on ourselves to live up to a certain way. After all, whom does it benefit?

I thought of 2 Corinthians 9:7: "Each of you should give what you have decided in your heart to give, not reluctantly or under compulsion, for God loves a cheerful giver." I decided to relate that to my current circumstance and give myself permission to do the cheats way instead of my usual way. After all, it mattered to me more that I had been able to care for people in that hour of need instead of baking, and it mattered to me even more that when my wonderful man arrived home, I was able to be in the moment with him instead of racing around the kitchen like a mad woman. So off to the supermarket I went; then when I got home, I put the chicken I'd had out for dinner in the fridge and declared it date night out.

I'm so glad that I'm learning, that I'm able to give myself permission to make the first things first and not worry about the others.

How about you? Are there times when you don't give yourself permission? Do you realize that the first needs to be first and that other things can fall to the wayside?

Embarrassed by Excellence: June 8, 2015

Picture, if you will, a thirteen-year-old me. I'd moved back to New Zealand and participated in my first World Vision forty-hour famine. In the lead up, I'd boldly gone up to teachers, people at church, and even strangers in the shops, asking them to sponsor me for a great cause. After the weekend of barley sugars and just juice had come and gone, assembly time at school came. On stage stood someone spouting off facts and figures; then my stomach churned, and my face felt hot as I heard my name mentioned. It turned out that my simple act of asking others had resulted in my raising a record figure and was being congratulated and used as an example.

For some reason, this attention embarrassed me; I didn't want to stand out. I didn't want to excel and be noticed. Rather, I wanted to snuff out what God had instilled. Because of that, when the next year's forty-hour famine came around, those in need missed out because I didn't want to deal with that again. That seems crazy, doesn't it? But how often do we get embarrassed by excellence and shrink back? Or even, for that matter, we miss out on what should be because fear of failure makes us shrink back? Both are just as detrimental. Sadly, I've got countless stories of just that on both counts.

This past week I've had God speak to my life on this matter in three ways (the homework during the week, the lecture on Friday, and then our friend preaching on Sunday). His speaking to me has got my mind ticking, and that is why once again I find myself with my fingertips tapping as I ask God to help me put to words the stirring in my heart.

Not all but many of us struggle with this. We allow the whispers of Satan, words those around us speak, or our own insecurities and hang-ups to win. Now, if we believe in God and trust that the Bible is the true Word of God, then why, oh why, do we allow this to happen time and again? Yes, there are verses about our sinful natures, the need for humility, putting others first, and so forth. But do we not need to balance those issues with the verses on God's purposing us for a deep, vibrant, and full life in Him? Should we reflect on the areas where God gifts people, where they excel, but in doing so reflect grace and point the glory due to Him, for He enables it after all? Is that not the kind of life we should lead? Well, that focus requires us to shrug off what has been and allow God to grow us; we would stand firm in the place He has planted our feet and not shrink back when the wave of embarrassment or whispers come.

Yesterday the Bible passage our friend visiting from the States shared at church was 1 Peter 1:3–9. The words spoken resonated with me deeply, as I also reflected on what I'd gleaned from the week's in-depth Bible study. I love how God used this to settle my heart, to assure me that it was okay to be the me He'd created me to be, to radiate Him as He grows me and uses me. For far too long,

I've battled with this tug-of-war, longing to grow deeper in Him but wanting to shrink back when His transforming power brings comments that embarrass me or are used to mock me.

I get change is not easy, especially when it's been our way for far too long. But I wonder if you too will ask God for help so you may boldly step out and excel where He's gifted you, called you, and purposed you. He also provides help to stay grounded and humble and to ensure He is the One receiving the "pat on the back."

I for one am going to ask God for such help. Instead of making excuses when the God-enabled joy and strength are noticed, I will delight in the work of my God. Instead of shrinking back when people notice I'm excelling and seem at ease with where God's planted me, I will rejoice at the ever-faithful hand of my God. Instead of retreating from the stepping-stones He is leading me to, I will seek His enabling to grow where I need to, to invest where I need to invest, and to have faith in all things where He has got me and will enable me. I will keep His Word anchored in my heart, so when my feet want to shuffle back, I can recall His truths and promises so they stay put.

How often do *you* try to snuff out what God has instilled in you out of fear and embarrassment?

Where could *you* be watching as others live out what God has for them and feel the tug to join?

Where could God be asking *you* to excel for Him?

What will be *your* response?

Bottled for All: June 10, 2015

It's true. I am so ridiculously happy despite some of the circumstances in my life being far from what I desire them to be.

Loved ones, friends, and even strangers see it. They notice the change that has taken place as I've grown in God.

Months had passed since my catching up with a friend, and she remarked on how happy I seem. She said I'd always been happy, but it's even more so. She said that if I could bottle it, I would make a fortune.

The beauty of it is that what many see is actually available to all. It's not some exclusive thing; rather, it's free for the taking for the masses. But it does require action. You can't be complacent about it.

When we believe in God, when we study His Word to know His character and ways, when we allow that knowledge to take root in our hearts to walk with Him to new levels, pursue growth, and display obedience, then our hearts can't help but overflow with joy like no other.

Psalm 28:7–8 amplified version says, "The Lord is my Strength and my [impenetrable] Shield; my heart trusts in, relies on, and confidently leans on Him, and I am helped; therefore my heart greatly rejoices, and with my song will I praise Him. The Lord is their [unyielding] Strength, and He is the Stronghold of salvation to [me] His anointed."

The question isn't, can you have that "bottled" goodness? It is, will you? So my friend, it's up to you.

Digging In: June 26, 2015

I've walked beside some people in the valley and others in their mountaintops of late. Today, as I took a moment out from business paper work and housework to sit in my special chair with phone in hand, I couldn't help but think of how timely the song playing was as I touched base with one in the valley (The song was "Can't Give Up Now" by Mary Mary).

As I put my phone down, I reflected on the words for myself. On many fronts of life, we may feel like we're taking one step forward and then another back. I've been praying and waiting for God on many things, and just when it seems like a door opens, it remains slightly ajar, with the glimmer of what's ahead dangling before me. Or in some cases, it slams shut. But what I really want is for the door to fling open so I'm able to race through it. I don't necessarily mean all doors at once, though truth be told, I'd love that, but at least one would be good.

It would be easy to feel deflated, to wonder just what God is doing, to feel like those things longed for and promised on an array of fronts just aren't going to come to pass. But as the song encourages, we can't turn back. So it's time to dig in that much more, to continue being expectant, patient, trusting, and accepting.

When it feels to us like God is taking forever, to Him the time is but a nanosecond. When we can see only a sliver of the picture, He sees the full picture and is the best person to have it in hand. I like to think that all these "almost" moments are going to be well worth the wait. What God unfolds is beyond my wildest dream, as has been the case so often.

Are you in a similar space in your life and need to dig in that much more? If so, where could you ask God to help you? Where do you need to dig into His presence and His Word to ensure you don't create your own doors, which bring too great a consequence and see you missing out on the door He's working on for you? I'm sure you don't want to give up now, just like I don't. So let's keep on digging in.

An August like No Other: August 9, 2015

Here we are in the month of August again, and in a matter of weeks, we see the eleven-year mark on this journey. However, the dread we've felt at the end of each July, the gnawing feeling I've had in the pit of my stomach on all the previous starts to this month, hasn't been there. What reminded me that it was indeed that time were people's questions about how I was doing, where we were on the journey, and so forth. If I'm honest, I'll admit that I felt some pressure to blog as the days ticked by. And while I sit at the computer, I do so not with pity or the wish to highlight that milestone but rather to proclaim the goodness of my God.

You see, all these years I've read verses in the Bible such as these:

Behold, I am doing a new thing! Now it springs forth; do you not perceive and know it and will you not give heed to it? I will even make a way in the wilderness and rivers in the desert. (Isa. 43:19)

I can do all things through Christ who strengthens me. (Phil. 4:13)

Then you will experience God's peace, which exceeds anything we can understand. His peace will guard your hearts and minds as you live in Christ Jesus. (Phil. 4:7)

I've not completely understood in the past how these verses could be the reality in the thick of life. But now I get it, and I know them to be true. God has captured my heart in such a way this year that He has completely transformed my life. While I'm still very much a work in progress, I have such freedom and joy like never before. I am content and at peace, and I know that with such certainty and Him as my anchor, I won't just be fine; I can flourish, even in the waiting and the unknown. There is fullness to life when it's truly lived with God.

I know that when I walk the path God has for me, it's the safest and best place to be. I also know that life happens, and Satan will go out of his way to steal the newfound gems with God. If only you could have seen our reality for the past few months to know that in sickness and turmoil, one thing piling on top of another, from small to big, that you can still experience all that. We've had major business sagas: my being sick for three weeks, utility vehicles smashed at the hands of another, thousands of dollars' worth of tools stolen, one appliance after another not working, progress delays for our home (and that's still only at paperwork stage and no where near building stage), confusion about what God is doing with where He has me, people pulling for us and wanting so much. The trials have been far from ideal. However, even in all that, while I've felt weary, I've still had freedom, joy, and peace because God is my anchor. I know His character; I'm hopeful and expectant. None of that changes with the ups and downs of life if we allow God and His Word to penetrate our hearts, minds, and lives to their fullness.

Call me crazy, but I still 100 percent believe that God has given us countless assurances that we will have our miracles. While the road is long, His hand is very much on us for all that's been and all that will be. I'm hopeful and expectant for so much in so many aspects of life, because I know the heart of my God, hear when He speaks, and know He is incapable of breaking a promise.

So what about you? What are you going through that makes you feel like this can't be your reality? Will you trust God with a little and see Him work it into a lot? Can you take your eyes off your problems and focus instead on God and His truths? Will you dare to live beyond what you can see to pursue what God sees?

Signing Off: September 10, 2015

It's hard to believe that it's been just over three years since the book launched and the blog took flight. In that time, I have met extraordinary people, walked beside special ladies in the trenches, and gotten a glimpse of just how big our God is and how great is the work He does in and through people.

I must admit that when things unfolded three years ago, I had full expectations that it wouldn't be long till we had our miracles in our arms. I would share the big news on here, and that was what changed things. But instead here I sit, closing the door on one chapter and embarking on the next, with it looking oh so different from anything I could have ever pictured.

What I've learned is that walking God's path for me is filled with untold joy and is such a privilege. It is far better than the one I had set before myself, because He is my maker and knows best. I can't lie and say I'm not daunted by what is ahead, uncertain how things will unfold. I have a feeling that each stepping-stone God has laid out for me is going to be that much scarier than the last. Yet I can go with full trust because of how intimately I know Him now because of what He has proved to me time and again.

So, my friends, at this juncture I can share that this blog is being formed into a second book and will soon be with the publishers in the States and likely be released in the New Year. This website, Twitter, and Facebook will soon be no more, marking an end of an era, if you will. God has me stepping up in some areas that feel a bit like boot camp for what lies beyond that. And when the time is right, the domain reserved for http://www.nataliahatton.com will come to life, and yet another chapter and unknown adventure will begin.

We may cross paths with my speaking at a women's event at your church, with your keeping an eye out for the next chapter's website and following things there, or maybe with our bumping into each other in the streets. Whatever the case may be, I wish to thank you from the bottom of my heart for those who have been brave enough to open up about their own journey and invite me in to walk alongside them. Here's special thanks to those who have followed us and cheered us on in the peaks and valleys, supporting me on many fronts.

At the Bible study where I'm a leader, there was a recent question about the priorities of our lives. After I pondered what my priorities were I wrote the answer, putting - God, Brett and pointing people to God. I am excited to be going through boot camp, coming out on the other side to proclaim how great my God is, in an even greater capacity, and being able to do what I love in pointing people to Him. So watch this space, people.

As I sign off, I again thank you greatly and wish you all the best in all that unfolds in your journey from here. May you see glimpses of how great God is and just how adventurous life can be if you watch for the path He lays before you. Obediently walk it, and allow yourself to skip and hop down it as you bask in the wonder of all He has for you. When we know Him and walk with Him, there is fullness like never before. So let's head off into all He has for us, my friends. Until our paths meet again.

NOTES

Unless otherwise noted, Scripture quotations are taken from the New International Version (NIV)

1   Blog - The Resounding Hope: March 11, 2013 – Woman of Faith, *Daily Gifts of Hope Devotional,* (Nashville TN: Thomas Nelson, 2012)
2   Blog - Thankful: April 5, 2013 – Woman of Faith, *Daily Gifts of Hope Devotional,* (Nashville TN: Thomas Nelson, 2012)
3   Blog – 'Tis the Season for Hope and Joy: December 8, 2013 – Woman of Faith, *Daily Gifts of Hope Devotional,* (Nashville TN: Thomas Nelson, 2012)
4   Blog – Tug-of-War: January, 28, 2014 – TD Jakes, *God's Leading Lady,* (Nashville TN: Thomas Nelson, 2004)

Printed in the United States
By Bookmasters